The Hive

The hive is thriving, at least that is what everyone believes.

Beneath the polished reports, constant productivity, and tightly controlled order, something dangerous has been growing unnoticed. When a mysterious illness begins spreading through the worker bees, fear moves quickly through the hive. Productivity drops. Trust erodes. Leadership responds with stricter control and deeper secrecy.

Blair, an ambitious worker bee with a sharp eye for inefficiencies, begins to realize the illness is only a symptom. Guided by an enigmatic butterfly known only as "Mentor," Blair uncovers a far greater threat buried deep within the hive itself: a culture built on fear, outdated governance, rigid hierarchies, and the illusion that stability means safety.

The Hive: Volume 1 is a psychological-thriller business fable that fuses edge-of-your-seat storytelling with powerful lessons in leadership, culture, governance, risk, and compliance. Through a unique dual-layer structure, the story pulls readers into the drama of the hive while connecting its struggles to real-world challenges facing modern organizations navigating disruption, transformation, cybersecurity, and trust.

For leaders, risk professionals, technologists, and emerging changemakers, this is a story about what happens when organizations stop listening long before they stop functioning.

The most dangerous risks are the ones hidden inside systems people believe are working.

Security, Audit and Leadership Series

Series Editor: Dan Swanson, Dan Swanson and Associates, Ltd., Winnipeg, Manitoba, Canada.

About the Book Series

The scope and mandate for cybersecurity and internal audit continues to evolve each year, as does the complexity of the business environment and speed of the changing risk landscape in which it must operate. The fundamental goal of this exciting series is to produce leading-edge books on critical subjects facing security and audit executives and practitioners. Key topics addressed include Leadership, Cybersecurity, Security Leadership, Privacy, Strategic Risk Management, Auditing IT and Technology, and Audit Management and Leadership.

If you're interested in submitting a proposal for a book to be included in the series, please email the series editor, Dan Swanson: dswanson_2008@yahoo.ca

Relevant Impact: A Field Guide to Integrated Assurance
By Patrick M. Hayes

Cybersecurity and the Art of Cyberwar
By Dan Shoemaker, Tamara Shoemaker, and Amir Jabri

Trust Hacked: What Firewalls, Failures, and the Frontlines Taught Me About Trust
By Nia Luckey

Organizational Resilience & Artificial Intelligence: A Practical Framework for Crisis Leadership, Adaptability & Sustainable Performance
By Arnab Mukherjee and Sachin Kumar

Mission-Critical Governance: Focusing on What Matters Most
By Tim J. Leech

Governing AI Risk—The RIVER Charter: An Enterprise Resilience Standard
By Alex Golbin

Cloud Compliance Essentials: How to Build and Maintain Market Access in the B2B CSP Ecosystem
By Forrest R. Foster

AI-Driven Decision-Making in Finance
Edited by Dr. Bilal Bagis

The CISO Playbook: The Adversarial Mindset
By Andres Andreu and Hector Monsegur

The Hive: A Fable of Fear, Governance and Transformation, Volume 1
By Brian Albertson

The Hive: A Fable of Fear, Governance and Transformation, Volume 2
By Brian Albertson

The Hive
A Fable of Fear, Governance and Transformation, Volume 1

A Psychological Thriller Business Fable on Leadership, Culture and GRC

Brian Albertson

CRC Press
Taylor & Francis Group
Boca Raton London New York

CRC Press is an imprint of the
Taylor & Francis Group, an **informa** business

Designed cover image: Shutterstock ID: 2756092009

First edition published 2027
by CRC Press
2385 NW Executive Center Drive, Suite 320, Boca Raton FL 33431

and by CRC Press
4 Park Square, Milton Park, Abingdon, Oxon, OX14 4RN

CRC Press is an imprint of Taylor & Francis Group, LLC

ISBN: 9781041236443 (hbk)
ISBN: 9781041240860 (pbk)
ISBN: 9781003740056 (ebk)

DOI: 10.1201/9781003740056

Typeset in Caslon
by KnowledgeWorks Global Ltd.

Contents

About the Author

Brian Albertson is a technology and governance leader, mentor, and storyteller with more than 25 years of experience across IT, cybersecurity, governance, risk, compliance, operations, and transformation. Throughout his career, he has focused on helping people solve hard problems, simplify complexity, and build practical ways of working that last.

He currently serves in an architecture and governance role within a Fortune 50 company, where his work centers on improving how organizations manage controls, risk, accountability, and change. Brian is known for taking complex topics and explaining them in ways people can understand and use.

Outside of work, Brian has a long history of serving in the community. A recent example is leading the ISACA Atlanta Chapter through its transformation. He has worked to support members, students, volunteers, and companies across the Atlanta area, Southeast, US, and more. He cares deeply about mentorship, opening doors for others, and helping the next generation grow in both skill and confidence.

Brian believes many problems in business and technology are not caused by a lack of talent, but by unclear ownership, poor communication, weak follow-through, and systems that drift over time. He also believes good leadership is often simple: listen well, serve others, tell the truth, and keep improving.

At the core of his work is a simple goal: serve people, develop people, and deliver results.

Preface

This book exists because too many things that should be simple have been made hard.

Most people reading this are already doing the work. You are leading teams. You are making decisions. You are dealing with governance, risk, technology, and change every day. The problem is not effort or intent. The problem is that over time we have added layers that create confusion instead of clarity.

I did not write this book to introduce a new model or sell an idea. I wrote it because I have watched capable people slow down not because the work was difficult but because the way we explain it no longer matches how work gets done.

This book is about clarity.

It is also meant to be a fun read.

I have always learned more when I was enjoying what I was working on. When things feel heavy, people disengage. When ideas are approachable and even a little enjoyable, they stick. That is intentional here. This book is meant to be useful, but it is also meant to be something you want to keep reading.

There is also a personal reason this book took the shape it did.

In 2017, I was helping someone cut their grass when I was attacked by bees. What started as a simple act turned into a moment that nearly ended my life. At the time, it felt overwhelming. Everything happened at once. Nothing made sense. I did not even realize I was using bees and what happened to me to explain this work until after I completed the first draft of the book.

It was not until I finished writing this book that I realized something important. One of my greatest adversaries became my greatest teacher.

That realization changed how I think about this work. It is not just about systems or structure. It is about people. It is about helping people connect to one another, grow with confidence, and realize their goals and dreams without unnecessary friction in the way.

I have been fortunate to have several amazing mentors in my life. The first were my mom and dad, Linda and Robert Albertson. They lived lives rooted in service. They taught me early that helping others is not optional. It is the work. They showed me that leadership starts with care, listening, and a willingness to step in when someone needs help.

On top of that are two huge supporters, Susan and Leon. Thank you for everything you did to make this book a reality.

Also like to thank the many others influenced me along the way, but that foundation never changed. Serve people. Develop people. Help them move forward.

That belief runs through every page of this book.

Bees are not random. They have structure. They have roles. They have purpose. Each part matters. When you do not understand that order, it looks like chaos. When you do, it becomes clear that order is what allows things to work.

The same is true in organizations and in the systems we build. What we often call complexity is really a lack of shared understanding. When roles are clear, purpose is known, and decisions are grounded, work moves faster, not slower.

This book challenges the status quo, but it does so with care. It is not about tearing things down. It is about questioning what no longer serves us and simplifying where we can without losing what matters.

If you are looking for theory, this is not that book. If you are looking for practical ways to think, decide, and lead with more confidence, this book was written for you.

My hope is that you read this book and take what you need from it. Use it to bring clarity to your work. Enjoy the process along the way.

And if it helps you move forward, consider paying that forward. Help someone at work. Help someone in your community. Help a team that feels stuck.

Sometimes progress starts with structure. Sometimes it starts with a conversation. Often it starts with simply showing up for someone else.

Thank you for taking the time to read this.

I hope you enjoy the book.

AI Usage Statement

I made limited use of OpenAI ChatGPT-5 during the drafting of this book. It helped with early brainstorming, sharpening a few section headings, and offering ideas for how to better organize parts of the manuscript. The thinking, judgment, and final wording are mine, and I take full responsibility for the finished work.

1
The Discontented Hive

The next morning began with the soft tone that signaled the first flight. Bees unfolded from their cells and gathered in lanes like staff arriving for the early shift. The air was cool, not cold, but the chill lingered a little longer than usual. Blair noticed it as she flexed her wings. She told herself it was nothing, then felt the same thought echo inside many minds around her. Too many small things had begun to feel like nothing. Too many small things were adding up.

The overseers stood at the end of each lane with clipboards and ink pads. They nodded without warmth and checked names as workers approached for assignment. The wall behind them held a wax map of fields, a grid of squares with small pins that showed routes. Someone had labeled it Route Map Seven A in confident letters. Two red pins sat in the same square as if they were arguing quietly. Blair studied that square for a moment, then stepped forward.

"Assignment," the overseer said without looking up.

"Fourteen," Blair replied.

The overseer pressed a stamp against the paper on his board. "Attest," he said, and pointed at the square where she should sign. His tone made the act feel like a ritual rather than a confirmation of reality. She signed. The ink was dull.

"Question," Blair said respectfully. "Fourteen overlapped with Nine yesterday. We had three collisions in the east meadow. If we stagger the lanes, we can cover more ground and avoid the turns that slow us down."

The overseer glanced up as if forced to acknowledge a sound he did not like. "Your role is to fly Fourteen. Route design is handled by the council. If you are tired, request leave."

"I am not tired," Blair said. "I am looking at the map."

"Then fly Fourteen," he said, and looked past her to the next worker. "Attest."

DOI: 10.1201/9781003740056-1

Blair moved on. She felt the eyes of a younger bee on her. The young one, barely through her first season, shifted in place with the nervous energy of a trainee. Blair remembered being that new. The rules felt like safety then. With time, they began to feel like barriers that were quietly closing in.

Outside, the fields were bright. The first light touched the flowers, and the air smelled clean. Blair breathed it in and tried to clear the fog she had felt inside the hive. She launched, tilted into the familiar pattern of Fourteen, then adjusted, not enough to break a rule outright, but enough to avoid the old collision path. A few other workers mirrored her correction without discussing it. Small acts of sense-making did not need approval. They needed courage.

She passed Karo near the first turn. Karo's wingbeats stuttered. His legs shook under the weight of a full load that should not have taxed him. He looked embarrassed more than worried.

"You good," Blair asked.

"I am fine," he said. "I just did not sleep well."

He said it as if he were explaining a small, temporary glitch. He said it the way many had begun to explain a growing fog. Blair watched him settle on a flower and rest for a moment. He would force himself to keep up because that was what the hive taught them to do.

By mid-morning, the lanes were crowded. Two workers drifted into each other near the orchard wall. A third overcompensated and clipped a thorn. No one was seriously hurt, but the stutter in the pattern cost minutes. The overseers would file a report, and the report would recommend another form to prevent future collisions. Blair could see it before it happened.

When she returned with her first load, the staging area buzzed with the energy of an inspection. Overseers had set up tables for signatures and spot checks. They weighed loads with careful ceremony. They asked questions that sounded correct without changing anything. One held a tiny ruler to measure the width of a comb line. Another tapped a log with the tip of his stylus as if hunting for a misprint that could be written up as a finding.

Sera stood in front of the table with a load that glittered with clear light. It should have been amber. The overseer frowned.

"What is this," he asked.

"Nectar from the white clover," Sera said, and blinked as if her eyes were slow to focus.

"This appears thin," the overseer said. "You should verify viscosity at the source."

Sera nodded, then swayed. Blair moved closer and steadied her with a wingtip. The overseer noticed the motion but marked only the log. Sera whispered thanks and tried to smile. The smile trembled.

Blair delivered her load and stepped back into the lane. The young trainee from earlier appeared at her side and spoke in a low voice.

"I am Pip," she said. "Can I ask you something."

"Ask," Blair said.

"Do you really talk to overseers like that," Pip asked. "I would not know what to do if they looked at me the way that one looked at you."

"I talk when something matters," Blair said. "Not because I enjoy conflict. I will show you the fields later. The map is helpful, and the flowers tell the truth."

"The flowers tell the truth," Pip repeated. She liked the way that sounded. "What about the logs."

Blair looked at the moving line of workers and the neat stacks of paper. "Logs are supposed to tell the truth. Sometimes they tell a story that fits a rule instead."

Pip nodded slowly. "Is that allowed."

"It is common," Blair said, and the answer felt heavier than it should have.

By midday, the sun was warm. The fields roared with life. Blair found a rhythm and let her body do what it knew. She fell into a series of efficient circles that felt like music. When she flew like this, she remembered why she had joined the hive. The world outside was generous. The work had a purpose that did not need to be spoken. She tasted the nectar on her tongue and thought of the honey that would last through nights and storms. She let that feeling push back against the numb efficiency inside the walls.

Not far away, near the old stone marker at the edge of the meadow, something flickered in the light. Blair caught a glimpse of colors that did not belong to a bee at all. It was small, then it was gone, as if the air had folded around it. It left a dart of curiosity in her mind and a thin trace of scent that she could not place. She considered circling to

The overseer turned the polished look on her. "Record shows you have raised process questions two days in a row."

"I will keep doing that until they are answered," Blair said evenly.

The overseer marked a line on his board and said nothing else. Blair stayed with Karo until his breathing slowed, then helped him return. She knew the citation would follow him even if he recovered. Mistakes in a system like this stayed on paper longer than they stayed in a body.

By midday, the mist burned away and the heat returned. The scent in the hive thickened again as the day wore on. Blair carried a load to storage and stopped short. The combs near the east wall had sagged a fraction of an inch. It was not dramatic, but it was enough to change the angle of a few cells. Honey glistened at the edges where it should have sealed cleanly. An engineer would see it. An overseer would call it within tolerance. Blair felt Sable's words in her ears. When the walls hum wrong, it is time to listen.

She found an engineer named Ilex near the pumps and asked him to look at the wall. Ilex was thoughtful and careful, a bee who did not waste words.

He ran a tool along the wax and frowned. "You have a good eye," he said. "The heat distribution is off. The balance is shifting."

"Can you fix it," Blair asked.

"I can adjust the vents," he said. "The structural fix requires approval. There is a backlog."

"How long," Blair asked.

"A few cycles," Ilex said. "Maybe more."

"What happens if we wait," Blair asked.

"We risk a slump," Ilex said. "Not a collapse. A slump forces a lot of rework. Rework is the word they use when they mean costs we pretend not to count."

He smiled without humor. "Thank you for saying something. Most only say something after a slump."

"Most do not want to be noticed," Blair said.

"Noticing can be a dangerous habit," Ilex said. "Keep it."

The day ended with another forum. This time the overseers invited questions. Blair considered asking about the wall, then decided to try a different route. She found Sable again, and together they made a small plan that did not require anyone to be called wrong in public.

"Nectar from the white clover," Sera said, and blinked as if her eyes were slow to focus.

"This appears thin," the overseer said. "You should verify viscosity at the source."

Sera nodded, then swayed. Blair moved closer and steadied her with a wingtip. The overseer noticed the motion but marked only the log. Sera whispered thanks and tried to smile. The smile trembled.

Blair delivered her load and stepped back into the lane. The young trainee from earlier appeared at her side and spoke in a low voice.

"I am Pip," she said. "Can I ask you something."

"Ask," Blair said.

"Do you really talk to overseers like that," Pip asked. "I would not know what to do if they looked at me the way that one looked at you."

"I talk when something matters," Blair said. "Not because I enjoy conflict. I will show you the fields later. The map is helpful, and the flowers tell the truth."

"The flowers tell the truth," Pip repeated. She liked the way that sounded. "What about the logs."

Blair looked at the moving line of workers and the neat stacks of paper. "Logs are supposed to tell the truth. Sometimes they tell a story that fits a rule instead."

Pip nodded slowly. "Is that allowed."

"It is common," Blair said, and the answer felt heavier than it should have.

By midday, the sun was warm. The fields roared with life. Blair found a rhythm and let her body do what it knew. She fell into a series of efficient circles that felt like music. When she flew like this, she remembered why she had joined the hive. The world outside was generous. The work had a purpose that did not need to be spoken. She tasted the nectar on her tongue and thought of the honey that would last through nights and storms. She let that feeling push back against the numb efficiency inside the walls.

Not far away, near the old stone marker at the edge of the meadow, something flickered in the light. Blair caught a glimpse of colors that did not belong to a bee at all. It was small, then it was gone, as if the air had folded around it. It left a dart of curiosity in her mind and a thin trace of scent that she could not place. She considered circling to look again, then returned to the lane. The hive did not tolerate wandering. The hive measured routes.

In the afternoon, the queen delivered a message through the channel that carried official speech. Her voice rolled through the chambers with practiced resonance. She praised tradition. She warned against distraction. She announced a program with a title that sounded like ceremony. Each worker would attest to five checks before each flight, then attest again upon return. The phrase five checks lodged in the air. It was a new ritual wrapped in the language of assurance.

Blair listened and felt the lane slow around her. A few workers looked up as if they could see the queen through the walls. Most kept moving. They had heard many programs announced this season. The programs changed names like the fields changed flowers. The work stayed the same. The new rule would add a few minutes to each shift. Those minutes would pile up and squeeze the day.

After the message ended, the overseers adjusted their tables to align with the new requirement. They added three new forms. They asked for two more signatures. They congratulated each other quietly for acting with speed. Blair watched them and imagined a different kind of speed, the kind that came from removing something that does not help. She shook off the thought. She had work to do.

As the sun lowered, the air inside the hive grew warm and thick. The combs smelled rich and sweet. It should have felt like comfort, but the warmth seemed to concentrate the strange fatigue that had drifted through the hive. Karo returned with his last load and stopped near the entrance to rest. His breathing was shallow. A tremor moved through his legs in a rhythm that had nothing to do with effort. Blair walked to him and offered water from a shallow cell.

"Take a minute," she said.

"I will be fine," Karo replied, and accepted the water. He sat without arguing for once. "Do not tell the overseer. I do not need a note on my file."

"I will not," Blair said. She knew how quickly compassion could be misread as weakness. She also knew that concealment was becoming its own risk.

She returned to her lane and noticed an odd pattern on the floor. Thin lines of resin had been spread near two corridors as if someone had tried to seal a draft. It was a clumsy fix, not the work of the engineers who understood airflow. She touched one of the lines and felt a sticky drag. The scent was harsh. It reminded her of the sharp smell in the training wing last week when a small group had been sent there for extra instruction after failing a spot check. She thought of Sera's clear nectar and felt a quiet unease move through her.

Late in the day, the council announced an open forum. The queen would not take questions, but the overseers would share priorities. The forum gathered in the central chamber beneath the high honey walls. Blair stood in the back and watched as hundreds settled into rows. The overseers took positions on a platform and arranged their clipboards like shields. The lead overseer, a bee with a polished tone and a fondness for slogans, stepped forward.

"Our hive remains a model," he said. "We are safe because we document. We are strong because we comply. We are resilient because we do not tolerate deviation."

The words were smooth, each one placed with care. The crowd listened without moving. Blair watched their faces and saw the resigned agreement born of long repetition. The lead overseer lifted a hand for emphasis.

> We have heard rumors about tired wings and confusion in the lanes," he said. "We remind you that performance is a matter of discipline. Fatigue is managed through scheduling. Confusion is solved with training. Speak to your supervisor if you need support. Do not speculate. Do not spread misinformation. Do your part, and the hive will thrive.

The speech ended with polite applause. The overseers left the platform through a side passage with a sense of ceremonial duty fulfilled. The forum dissolved into low conversation. Blair stayed a moment longer, then walked the long way back to her station.

As she moved through the corridor that connected the central chamber to the storage wing, she passed the archive. Most bees never entered it. It was a quiet place maintained by old workers who had once flown and now tended to records. The door stood slightly open. A soft light spilled through the gap. Something pulled her toward it, not curiosity for gossip, but a wish to understand how the hive had become so afraid of its own questions.

Inside, the air was cool and smelled of old wax. Tablets lined the walls, each one inscribed with charters, standards, and records of past seasons. An old bee sat behind a low desk with a small lamp. His eyes were milky at the edges but clear at the center. He looked up and smiled with a kindness that did not feel fragile.

"Evening," he said. "You are far from the lanes."

"I did not mean to intrude," Blair said. "I saw the light."

"Good," he said. "Most do not see it. They rush past, and light becomes a rumor. I am Sable. Sit if you wish."

Blair sat. The chair was a simple piece of comb shaped to hold a body that had worked and now rested. Sable turned a tablet so she could see it.

"This is the charter that founded our council," he said. "Do not worry, I will not recite it. I have found that recitation can be a kind of sleep."

Blair smiled despite her mood. "Did they always patrol the way they do now."

"No," Sable said.

> There was a time when a council listened more than it inspected. The hive got hurt, badly, and fear took root. Fear is a plant that grows quickly in the shade of a throne. It promises safety if you let it climb. It wraps around everything.

"Why do we still let it," Blair asked.

"Because some fear is useful," Sable said. "We remember the hurt and forget the lessons. We keep the rituals and forget the meaning. It takes energy to remember. It takes courage to ask who we want to be. It is easier to measure than to decide."

He looked at her for a long moment. "You have the look of one who still decides."

"I am not important," Blair said.

"Importance is a word for speeches," Sable said. "Decisions are made by the ones who show up."

Blair nodded and felt a quiet strength settle in her chest. She thanked him and stood to leave. As she reached the door, Sable spoke again.

"If you hear a new sound at night, do not ignore it. The hive speaks in ways that reports cannot. When the walls hum wrong, it is time to listen."

Back in the corridor, Blair felt the floors tremble slightly. It was not an earthquake. It was the long vibration of many bodies adjusting to a shared weight. She told herself Sable had planted the idea in her mind. Then she realized she was grateful for the reminder to listen.

The next day began with a dull gray light. A thin mist hung over the meadow. Flight would be safe but slower. The overseers added a weather form to the table. Blair watched them fit the new paper into the stack with satisfaction, as if the act itself could keep the mist from touching wings.

Pip met Blair near the entrance. "You said you would show me the fields," she said. "I have my first solo today."

"Good," Blair said. "We will fly together to the mark, then you take the lane. Remember, the map helps. The flowers tell the truth. If something looks wrong, trust what you see, then find a way to be right within it."

Pip repeated the words softly and stood a little taller. Together they launched into the gray light. The air smelled like damp morning. The mist beaded on their wings, then scattered in flight. At the mark, Blair peeled away and watched Pip settle into her route. The young bee kept a steady path and looked ahead rather than down at the invisible expectations she carried. Blair felt a small surge of pride. The hive was a place of rules, but it was also a place where people learned from each other. That hope was worth holding.

On her second circuit, Blair noticed a small crowd near the far edge of the meadow. Two overseers hovered over a bee who sat on the ground with his head low. It was Karo. He had not fallen. He had landed without finishing his lane. His breathing looked shallow again.

"What happened," Blair asked as she approached.

"Worker terminated route without authorization," one overseer said. "We will note the deviation and send him for training."

"I could not see the lane break," Karo whispered. "It blurred."

"You are fatigued," the overseer said. "You should have requested leave."

Karo nodded as if he wanted to give the correct answer. Blair felt heat rise in her chest.

"He needs a rest and a check," she said. "Not a citation."

The overseer turned the polished look on her. "Record shows you have raised process questions two days in a row."

"I will keep doing that until they are answered," Blair said evenly.

The overseer marked a line on his board and said nothing else. Blair stayed with Karo until his breathing slowed, then helped him return. She knew the citation would follow him even if he recovered. Mistakes in a system like this stayed on paper longer than they stayed in a body.

By midday, the mist burned away and the heat returned. The scent in the hive thickened again as the day wore on. Blair carried a load to storage and stopped short. The combs near the east wall had sagged a fraction of an inch. It was not dramatic, but it was enough to change the angle of a few cells. Honey glistened at the edges where it should have sealed cleanly. An engineer would see it. An overseer would call it within tolerance. Blair felt Sable's words in her ears. When the walls hum wrong, it is time to listen.

She found an engineer named Ilex near the pumps and asked him to look at the wall. Ilex was thoughtful and careful, a bee who did not waste words.

He ran a tool along the wax and frowned. "You have a good eye," he said. "The heat distribution is off. The balance is shifting."

"Can you fix it," Blair asked.

"I can adjust the vents," he said. "The structural fix requires approval. There is a backlog."

"How long," Blair asked.

"A few cycles," Ilex said. "Maybe more."

"What happens if we wait," Blair asked.

"We risk a slump," Ilex said. "Not a collapse. A slump forces a lot of rework. Rework is the word they use when they mean costs we pretend not to count."

He smiled without humor. "Thank you for saying something. Most only say something after a slump."

"Most do not want to be noticed," Blair said.

"Noticing can be a dangerous habit," Ilex said. "Keep it."

The day ended with another forum. This time the overseers invited questions. Blair considered asking about the wall, then decided to try a different route. She found Sable again, and together they made a small plan that did not require anyone to be called wrong in public.

Sable would pull the record of similar slumps from prior seasons. Ilex would write a quiet recommendation for a preventive fix and frame it as alignment with a policy the council still admired in principle. Blair would recruit a few respected workers to endorse the change to protect output. It was not a revolt. It was an attempt to move something that had stuck.

That night the hive sounded strange again. The hum stuttered, then caught, then stuttered. Blair could feel it in the walls of her cell. She lay awake and listened as small changes in the chorus of wingbeats rose and fell. In the distance, a faint scratch echoed, then stopped. She told herself it was the sound of rebalancing, nothing more. She slept lightly.

Before dawn, a guard from the storage wing ran a message through the channel. A section of comb near the east wall had drooped. It had not broken completely, but it had forced a fast shift in two rows and spilled a small river of honey that had to be caught before it wasted. No one was hurt. The overseers called it a near miss. The workers who cleaned it up called it a warning.

Ilex worked without pause for three hours. He coordinated vents and assigned crews to firm the wall. He did not waste time with speeches. By mid-morning, the wall held. The spill was contained. The overseers congratulated the crews on their response times and assigned two more forms to memorialize the event. The council sent a message praising resilience. No one mentioned the recommendation Ilex had submitted the previous afternoon. It was still in review.

Pip found Blair near the east corridor and stood very straight, as if her small body could hold a larger resolve.

"I heard about the wall," she said. "I saw the cleanup. I also heard that you asked for the fix yesterday."

"Ilex asked," Blair said. "I noticed. Many helped."

Pip nodded and looked toward the wall. "I do not understand why we always wait."

"Because waiting looks safe," Blair said. "There is no signature required to wait."

Pip was quiet for a moment. "I want to be the kind of bee who sees the wall before it droops," she said.

"You will be," Blair said. "Keep flying. Keep looking. Keep asking."

In the afternoon, Blair returned to the meadow. The light was clear. The scent of clover mingled with a thin trace of something sharp that she could not place. Near the old stone marker, she saw the flicker again. Colors that did not belong moved with an ease that looked like thought. A small figure perched on the edge of a leaf and seemed to watch the lanes with interest rather than judgment. When Blair turned fully toward it, the figure lifted gently and rose into the light with a slow cadence that looked like patience given wings. She felt a small, unexpected lift in her chest. Not hope exactly, more like recognition without understanding why.

She did not follow. She finished her lane, then took a longer way back that happened to pass near the old marker. There, in the curve of a petal, she found a tiny scale that shimmered like paint. It felt like the world had left a note.

She tucked the scale into a seam of wax near her cell. She did not know why. She did not think of omens and signs. She thought only of the way the figure had watched and the way her own attention had sharpened under that gaze.

That evening the queen announced another improvement. A central team would standardize flight checklists to remove variation. The new checklists would be printed on heavier wax to last longer. The overseers applauded. The workers repeated the new steps and practiced the order until the steps sang like a rhyme they could not forget. Blair completed the steps with accuracy. Then she sat with Sable and Ilex near the archive table and reviewed the list of past slumps.

"There," Sable said, and tapped a date. "See the pattern."

Blair read the notes. Heat spikes. Vent delays. Extra forms announced in the same window. A small increase in errors. A minor illness not recognized. She looked up and felt the room tilt a fraction. The pattern was not proof, but it was loud enough to demand an answer.

"We can show this to the council," Ilex said. "They will thank us and add another form."

"Not if we make it about output," Blair said.

> We tell a simple story. The wall droops when the hive is tired and hot. Both get worse when we slow workers with rituals that do not help. We propose a pilot to remove one burden and add one guard. We will use their favorite words. We will say control objective. We will say risk mitigation. We will say evidence of effectiveness.

Sable chuckled softly. "You speak their language without letting it speak you."

Blair smiled. "I want them to hear us. If their language is the bridge, I will walk it."

They wrote a one-page proposal without flourish. Ilex attached cooler data and heat maps. Sable added one line from an old charter that valued prevention over theater. Blair listed the names of five workers who agreed to try the pilot. She kept the list short and chose names the overseers respected. The proposal did not accuse. It invited.

The next day, the council did not reply. On the second, a deputy sent a note that asked three questions about the format of the data. On the third, a clerk returned the proposal with a request to route it through a different team for alignment. Blair felt frustration rise, then let it settle into a steady patience. Sable looked at her with approval she did not need. Ilex adjusted the vents again and refused to give up on a fix that made sense.

While they waited, the illness that no one would name rippled through the hive like a draft. A few bees missed shifts without explanation. A few returned from the fields with eyes that could not find the lane. Sera's hands shook when she tried to pour a cell. Pip slept an extra hour and woke ashamed. The overseers reminded everyone to hydrate and train. The council announced an initiative to celebrate resilience. The word resilience began to taste like a sweet syrup poured over everything until the shape beneath could not be seen.

Blair worked and watched. She asked quietly and listened hard. She kept notes that described what she saw, not what she was told to see. She shared them with Sable, who kept them safe in the archive. She visited Karo and made him laugh by telling stories that were funny because they were true. She flew with Pip at dawn and let the meadow teach both what mattered.

On a late afternoon near the end of the cycle, a shout rolled through the east corridor. A small group had stumbled in the lanes. No one was broken. The incident should have been minor. But a tremor passed through the hive at the same moment. The wall that had sagged earlier flexed again. The crews moved fast. Ilex pushed his tools and ordered the vents to open. Honey slid a fraction and held.

Blair stood near the edge and looked outward through a gap where the light cut the comb like a blade. The fields glowed with that late day fire that made everything look honest. On a tall stem, the small figure with impossible colors watched again. There was curiosity in the way it tilted its head, compassion in the way it did not rush forward. Blair felt the sense of being seen without being judged. She knew then that she was not alone in her noticing.

Inside, a bell rang for a council message. The queen's voice filled the air with calm certainty. She thanked crews for their speed. She reminded the hive that strength came from order. She pledged a new layer of checks to ensure nothing like this ever happened again. Blair listened to the familiar rhythm and felt a different rhythm rise beneath it, the quiet insistence of a truth that had waited long enough.

When the message ended, she walked to her cell and touched the tiny scale she had hidden in the wax. It caught the light like a small flame. She thought of Sable's advice to listen, of Ilex's quiet resolve, of Pip's careful courage, of Karo's weary smile. She thought of the wall and the mist and the map with the two red pins that argued with each other but never moved. She thought of her own voice, small inside a hive that believed size proved rightness.

She did not know the name of the figure in the field. She did not yet know what she would ask or what she would dare. She knew only this. The hive was tired. The hive was afraid. The hive had lost sight of why it worked at all. Her chest felt light and heavy at the same time, as if something had been taken away and something else had been given.

That night she lay awake and listened again. The hum rose and fell, then began to settle into a steadier tone as the vents equalized. The tremor eased. The walls grew quiet. She felt a calm she did not trust. Calm without change was a pause, not safety.

Near the edge of sleep, she heard a sound that did not belong to bees. A soft brush of wings like paper over silk. It moved once, then stilled. When she opened her eyes, the night was ordinary. She smiled into the dark, not because she felt safe, but because she felt ready.

Morning would come. The fields would wait. The overseers would arrange their clipboards and request signatures. The council would announce something with a proud title. The hive would move as it always had, and yet, something in the rhythm had shifted. A space had opened where a question could live.

Blair rose before the tone and walked toward the entrance without hurry. The air held a cool promise. At the threshold, she paused. The meadow spread out like a canvas for choice. On the far stem, color flickered once, as if a small hand had lifted to greet her. She breathed in, steadied her wings, and launched.

She did not know it yet, but the next step would bring her into a conversation that would change everything.

2
The Mysterious Mentor

Blair rose before the hive's morning tone, wings steady, the faint shimmer of color from the meadow still lodged in her thoughts. The overseers would soon arrange their clipboards, the queen would issue decrees, and the workers would march as they always had. Yet Blair could no longer shake the image of that figure glowing with impossible hues. She told herself she would not look for it, but her path bent toward the meadow as though the choice had already been made.

The flowers glistened with dew, droplets catching the first light like shards of glass. Workers busied themselves in rigid lanes, their flight paths carved by overseer decree, every wingbeat subject to inspection. Blair traced her own lane but slowed as she neared the far edge. She felt the tug of curiosity, the dangerous pull of something unsanctioned. Then she saw it: the figure again, perched upon a tall stem, wings shimmering with layered colors that seemed to hold the whole spectrum of dawn.

This time, the figure moved. It rose in a slow arc, drifted forward, and hovered before her with a composure that made the air itself seem calm. Its eyes met hers with patient recognition, as if it had been waiting.

"What do you notice?" it asked, voice clear and unhurried.

Blair startled at the question. She had expected riddles or commands, not something so simple, so piercing. She thought of her hive: resin smeared across walls where true repairs had been ignored, logs stacked higher than combs, overseers clutching their clipboards like shields. She thought of Karo's trembling legs, Sera's blurred eyes, Pip's whispered doubts.

"I notice fatigue," Blair said finally. "I notice fear. I notice walls patched with resin but never mended."

The figure tilted its head, as if weighing the answer. "And what story are you telling yourself about those things?"

 DOI: 10.1201/9781003740056-2

Blair hesitated. Few in the hive spoke of stories; they spoke of rules, measures, compliance. But she remembered Sable in the archive, reminding her that fear itself could become a story if repeated long enough. "That our hive is strong in appearance but brittle in truth," she said. "That we govern the wrong things. That we measure what does not matter."

A faint shimmer pulsed along the figure's wings. "And if you could ask one question of your leaders, what would it be?"

Blair's chest tightened. She had so many questions pressing at her tongue—why do you not listen, why do you add weight instead of lifting it, why do you praise signatures while bees collapse? But when she opened her mouth, only one came out: "Why do you not see?"

The figure's voice softened. "Perhaps they see only what they choose to measure."

Blair frowned, frustration burning through her fatigue. "And what use is that? What good is a ledger if the hive collapses beneath it?"

The figure did not answer. Instead, it asked, "What are you willing to risk to learn the truth?"

The words struck deeper than she expected. Risk was a dangerous term inside the hive. Risk meant demotion, silence, being reassigned to meaningless tasks until one's wings stiffened and one's name faded. Yet as she hovered there in the meadow's light, she realized that not risking anything was already killing her hive slowly. Karo was breaking, Sera was trembling, Pip was doubting, and the walls themselves were beginning to sag.

"I will risk seeing," she whispered.

The figure's eyes glowed faintly, like embers under ash. "Then let us see together."

They spoke for what felt like hours, though the sun had hardly moved in the sky. The figure never lectured; it only questioned. Each question was like a mirror turned toward Blair's own mind.

"What matters most in your hive's survival?"

Blair answered automatically, "Discipline. Compliance. Efficiency."

"Whose words are those?" the figure asked gently.

Blair faltered. She realized they were not her own, but the queen's speeches echoing inside her.

"What happens when rituals replace meaning?" the figure continued.

Blair saw in her mind the overseers' endless forms, the resilience drills that left bees too exhausted to fly, the rituals that consumed hours without producing a drop of nectar. "Then we mistake movement for progress," she said.

The figure nodded slowly. "And who benefits from red tape, and who suffers?"

Blair thought of overseers congratulating one another for new inspection tables, while workers like Sera shook under scrutiny. "They benefit," she said bitterly. "And we suffer."

The figure's wings shimmered brighter, as if her honesty had weight. "Then ask yourself this—what must die for your hive to live?"

Blair flinched. The question cut deeper than any inspection ever had. Rituals had become sacred. To challenge them was to challenge the queen herself. Yet she knew the truth when she heard it: some rituals had to die if the hive was to survive.

The figure leaned closer. "Leadership is not holding tighter. It is knowing when to let go. Will you let go?"

Blair shook her head, overwhelmed. "I am one worker. I cannot decide what to let go."

"Every hive begins with one bee's decision to notice," the figure said. "To see. To name. That is where letting go begins."

Something inside Blair shifted—equal parts terror and liberation. For the first time, she realized her role was not to wait for the queen to change but to begin herself.

When she returned to the hive, her wings carried her differently. The halls smelled the same, the combs buzzed the same, but everything looked sharper, harsher. Overseers were announcing new inspections, new forms, new slogans plastered along honey walls. She realized suddenly that these were not immutable truths; they were choices, choices made by leaders who governed rituals rather than results.

Pip noticed the change first. "You look different," she whispered one evening.

Blair tried to smile. "Perhaps I am learning to see."

"And what do you see?"

Blair glanced around at the overseers bent over their clipboards, at the queues of workers waiting for signatures. "I see we are measuring our prison."

Pip's eyes widened. "Then what is freedom?"

Blair hesitated, the word dangerous even in thought. "Perhaps freedom is choosing what truly matters," she said softly. "I am still learning."

Blair did not sleep well that night. The hum of the hive seemed louder, less harmonious, filled with small stutters she had never noticed before. She thought of Sable's warning: *when the walls hum wrong, it is time to listen.* She closed her eyes, but the sound followed her into restless dreams.

In the morning, the overseers announced a new requirement: five additional checks before each flight. They spoke as though the words were gifts, as if the forms themselves could strengthen wings. Blair watched the line of workers slump at the news, shoulders bent under the invisible weight. The overseers congratulated themselves on the "speed of implementation," while the fields outside waited for bees too weary to reach them.

Pip shifted nervously beside Blair. "Five more checks? I can barely keep up now."

"You will," Blair said gently. "But not because the checks make you strong. You'll keep up because you must."

Pip bit her lip. "Then what is the point?"

Blair had no answer. Not yet.

That afternoon, Blair sought the meadow again. The figure was waiting, perched calmly on a blossom that glowed as though the light itself bowed to it.

"You returned," the figure said.

"I had to," Blair admitted. "I see more now, but it makes me restless. My hive is drowning in rules. The queen calls it resilience, but all I see is exhaustion."

The figure nodded, unhurried. "Then let us ask again: what is resilience?"

Blair repeated the queen's decree. "Resilience is discipline. Compliance. Strength in rituals."

The figure's eyes narrowed slightly. "And is Karo resilient?"

Blair's heart clenched. She thought of his trembling legs, the way he forced himself to fly until his body gave way. "No. He is broken."

"And why is he broken?"

"Because he feared to admit weakness," she whispered. "Because he carried more than he could bear."

The figure's wings pulsed, brighter now. "Then resilience is not resistance. Resilience is bending without breaking. It is strength that adapts, not strength that clings. What might resilience look like if your hive released rituals instead of adding them?"

The word *release* struck her like a forbidden scent. Release was dangerous, nearly heretical. Yet in her mind she imagined it: fewer inspections, fewer queues, more time in the fields, more space for rest. She saw Karo laughing again, Sera flying without trembling, Pip stepping into the sky without fear.

"It would look alive," Blair whispered.

The figure smiled faintly. "Then remember: leadership is not adding weight. It is knowing what to remove."

Inside the hive, new decrees cascaded daily. Posters inscribed with slogans—*Compliance is Strength, Resilience is Discipline*—lined the honey walls. Overseers added inspection tables at every corridor. The workers obeyed, but Blair noticed the subtle changes: wings beating slower, eyes dulled, humor rare.

Sera was fading fastest. Her legs shook as she poured nectar into cells. Once, Blair caught her whispering apologies to the comb itself, as if ashamed for not being enough.

"Rest," Blair urged quietly.

"I cannot," Sera murmured. "There is too much to sign."

Blair's chest ached. What good was a hive that measured signatures while its bees collapsed?

Ilex the engineer was one of the few who still spoke with quiet honesty. Blair found him near the vents, his tools laid out in careful rows.

"The east wall is slumping again," he said without looking up. "I can delay it with adjustments, but the structure needs more than patches."

"Does the council know?" Blair asked.

"They have my reports. They prefer forms to fixes." He glanced at her. "But you… you notice."

Blair hesitated, then whispered, "The mentor says governance is deciding what deserves attention. We govern rituals. We should govern results."

Ilex studied her, then gave a slow nod. "You may be right. But be careful. The overseers measure more than nectar—they measure loyalty."

At night, Blair met Pip in a quiet corner of the comb. The younger bee leaned close, eyes wide with curiosity.

"Tell me what you see in the meadow," Pip whispered.

Blair hesitated, but she saw hunger in the young one's gaze—the same hunger she herself carried. "I see a mentor. It asks questions no overseer dares ask."

"Like what?"

Blair recited them softly, as though the words themselves could draw punishment: *What do you notice. What story are you telling. What are you willing to risk.*

Pip repeated them, voice trembling. "They sound dangerous."

"They are," Blair said. "But they are also true."

The illness that had begun quietly now rippled through the hive. Workers missed shifts, some claiming fatigue, others simply vanishing into the combs. Overseers labeled it "temporary inefficiency," but Blair saw the truth: wings faltering, eyes dull, bodies too weary to rise.

The council responded with ceremony. They announced a new initiative, draped in the language of assurance: *The Resilience Campaign.* It required double attestations, mandatory drills, and daily declarations of loyalty.

Blair almost laughed at the absurdity. Bees who could barely stand were forced to recite oaths of strength. Logs multiplied like weeds, choking the hive with paper-thin rituals.

Sera collapsed one evening after inspection. Pip rushed to her side, panic in her eyes. Blair steadied Sera gently. The overseer noted the incident with his stylus but offered no aid.

"She will be fine," he said coldly. "Noncompliance breeds weakness."

Blair's wings trembled with restrained fury. "No," she whispered once he left. "Noncompliance is not weakness. Blindness is."

The next morning, Blair sought the meadow again. The mentor greeted her with a calm nod.

"You are troubled," it observed.

Blair's words spilled out, raw and unpolished. "My hive is collapsing under rituals. Sera can barely stand. Karo hides his weakness in shame. Pip trembles at every inspection. And still, they call it resilience."

The figure listened, wings shimmering softly. "Then what will you do?"

Blair's breath caught. "What can I do? I am one worker."

"One worker is enough," the figure said. "Governance begins with deciding what deserves attention. You cannot change the council today. But you can choose where you place your attention. Choose nectar over signatures. Choose life over ritual. Choose courage over silence."

Blair stared at it, chest heavy and light all at once. She realized then that seeing was not enough. Action, however small, was required.

That evening, Blair tried something dangerous. She and Pip skipped one of the new checks before flight. Instead of lining up for signatures, they launched straight into the meadow, wings free of delay.

The difference was immediate. Their circuits were faster, their loads heavier, their bodies less strained. When they returned, Pip's eyes glowed with exhilaration.

"We finished before the overseers even noticed," she whispered.

"Do you see?" Blair asked.

Pip nodded fiercely. "We measure our prison. But today, we measured freedom."

Word of Blair's small defiance did not travel loudly; it traveled in glances. A few workers noticed that she and Pip returned with heavier loads and clearer eyes. No one spoke of it near overseers, but the observation settled like pollen on minds hungry for something true. By evening, two more workers adjusted their routines—nothing overt, only a quiet tightening of flight patterns, a refusal to linger at inspection tables when the queue snaked down the corridor.

The overseers noticed numbers, not faces. They remarked on an uptick in output with the baffled pride of those who think a machine has improved itself. They responded the only way they knew—by proposing a new round of measurements to "capture the momentum." Clipboards multiplied.

Sera's condition muddied the moment. She rallied for a day, then slipped again. Her eyes flickered as if the room blinked around her. When she tried to pour a cell, nectar wobbled and streaked the comb like a tear. An overseer docked her for "spillage." He recorded the infraction with the bored precision of someone who had learned to feel nothing while writing everything.

"I need rest," Sera murmured to Blair.

"You need time," Blair said softly. "Time is not a luxury; it's a cost we refuse to price."

She helped Sera to a quiet alcove, away from the inspection lamps that made every tremor look like guilt. Pip stood guard with a seriousness that made her seem older. Ilex arrived with water and a vial of cool scent used by engineers when the vents overheated. He dabbed it near Sera's temples. The tiny kindness steadied the air.

"We can't keep patching bodies like we patch walls," Ilex said under his breath.

"We can't keep pretending patches are strategy," Blair replied.

Ilex's eyes flicked toward the corridor. "Careful."

"I am past careful," Blair said, then softened. "But not careless."

He nodded at that—an engineer's appreciation for precise distinctions.

The illness strengthened its quiet campaign. It rarely shouted; it simply took more. Workers forgot simple steps, flew the wrong lane for a breath, clipped a thorn, apologized to the floor. The council labeled it "seasonal variance." Their messages came wrapped in the satin language of control. *Variance will normalize with discipline. Deviation will be trained away. Resilience is the remedy.*

Blair felt anger rise like heat under the comb. Resilience, the word repeated until it lost meaning, had become a shield for inaction. She wanted to stand in the central chamber and tear down the banners that preached strength while bees sagged under them. Instead, she chose a smaller, sharper path.

"Pip," she said quietly, "tomorrow we'll try something more deliberate."

Pip straightened. "More deliberate than skipping a check?"

"Deliberate is different from daring," Blair said. "Daring is an impulse. Deliberate is design."

"What's the design?"

"We'll run a controlled route. Same lane, same time, twice—once with all checks, once with only the essential ones. We'll track output, strain, and error. Then we'll compare."

Pip blinked. "We'll… measure?"

"We'll measure what matters," Blair said. "Not signatures. Outcomes."

Pip smiled like a student who had finally been handed a tool instead of a rule.

They executed at dawn. The first run, under full ritual, dragged like a cart through syrup. The queue cost 11 minutes. The double attestation—first at the threshold, then mid-lane—cost another four. The inspection of a pouch latch that had not failed in three seasons took two. They recorded the strain—the way wings burned forty lengths sooner, the way focus thinned during the second attestation when an overseer quizzed Pip on the definition of "resilience" and interrupted her memory with his own. They logged the load: lower, though not by much. They logged the errors: none—compliance is careful, but careful is not free.

The second run felt like wind. The essential checks—wing integrity, latch, storm alert—took 90 seconds. They launched with the warmth of movement in their shoulders. They cut the powdery drift that always rose over the white clover, banked tight at the marker, and returned with cells that rang with nectar's weight. Strain dropped, output rose, error remained zero.

Numbers don't shout; they insist. Blair and Pip copied the results on a small slate and tucked it into the edge of a comb in Sable's archive. Sable's milky eyes sharpened as he read.

"You have done what councils claim to do," he murmured. "You have produced evidence."

"Evidence of effectiveness," Blair said, borrowing the council's favorite phrase.

Sable smiled. "They will try to change the question if they cannot change the answer."

"We will keep answering," Blair said.

Sable placed the slate on a shelf marked with a symbol few bees remembered: a simple circle with a small open gap. "This mark," he said, "once meant 'unfinished by choice.' It signaled work we kept open for revision because certainty is fragile. Then fear turned gaps into threats. We glued the circle shut and called it control."

Blair touched the gap with one finger. "Unfinished by choice," she repeated, tasting a different kind of strength.

The overseers, alerted by motion more than meaning, tightened presence near the lanes. Clipboards doubled-timed. An officer with a lacquered voice delivered a corridor lecture on "the danger of innovation without authorization." The word innovation made Blair's wings twitch. In their mouths, it meant a new form disguised as a new idea.

Pip stood beside her, reciting patience like a prayer. "Deliberate, not daring. Deliberate, not daring."

Sera approached, eyes clearer after a night of real sleep that Blair and Ilex had brokered with a friendly guard. "If they ask," Sera whispered, "I was aligning my ledger." She winked, a small return of the humor exhaustion had stolen.

"Ledger alignment is sacred," Pip deadpanned, and they almost laughed—almost, because just then the floor trembled.

It was the east wall again. Not a collapse—something subtler, the way a held breath leaks out of a crowded room. Ilex was there before anyone called. He ran his tool along the seam, listening more than touching. Overseers began to arrange caution placards in an eager fan, the way some bees set tables before food exists.

"Vents now," Ilex said to the nearest engineer. "Two points east, one north. And balance heat away from the sag."

"Approval?" the engineer asked, haunted by forms.

"Approval is watching honey on the floor," Ilex snapped. "Move."

The air shifted. The sag eased by a whisper. Honey did not spill; it only thought about it, then reconsidered. Ilex exhaled.

An overseer appeared with a stylus poised. "Record the response time," he said. "This near miss proves our resilience."

"It proves the vents," Ilex said flatly.

"It proves our drills," the overseer insisted.

"It proves physics," Ilex said, then caught Blair's eye and smoothed his voice. "It proves we should fix the wall."

The overseer scribbled the sentence "We responded swiftly" as if it were a spell against maintenance.

Blair felt something cold and bright click into place: language itself was a control. If you defined success as speed of reaction, the wall had to sag to justify your report. If you defined success as preventing the sag, reports thinned, and your clipboard looked light. So, the wall sagged again and again, feeding the story that fed the role that fed the title that fed the pride.

"Define success differently," the mentor had said in other words. "Govern something else."

That evening, Blair met the figure on the same tall stem. The sky had the milky hue of a day that hadn't finished deciding whether it would be kind.

"We measured," Blair said without greeting. "Twice. Ritual and essential. The numbers are clear."

"And what do they change?" the figure asked.

"They change me," Blair said. "They move me from belief to knowledge."

The figure's wings hummed, a pleased vibration. "Knowledge changes posture."

"It also paints a target," Blair said. "The overseers feel something moving. They respond with slogans. They think words can tighten bolts."

"Words can loosen them too," the figure said. "Tell a different story loudly enough and old bolts rattle out by themselves."

"How?" Blair asked, not out of ignorance but out of a careful appetite.

"Through parable," the figure replied. "Would you hear one?"

Blair nodded.

"There was a hive that measured its shadow at noon," the figure began. "Each day it marked the darkness on the ground and called the length a proof of strength. When drought came, the shadow shrank. They added forms to record the shrinking. When wind came, the shadow swung. They added drills to steady it. Then one day, a worker asked why they measured the ground at all when the combs were empty. The council replied that shadows were safer to measure because shadows could not spill."

Blair closed her eyes. "We measure what cannot hold weight because it cannot embarrass us."

"You govern what does not argue," the figure said softly. "And you call the silence compliance."

Silence lay between them like clear water. Blair saw her hive under that water—beautiful, distorted, struggling for air.

"What happens next?" she asked.

"You choose," the figure said. "You have run your first experiment. Run your second. Invite your third. Bring Ilex data he can wield. Bring Sable evidence he can archive. Bring Pip courage she can lend others. Quiet acts accumulate. Fear feeds on spectacle; change feeds on sequence."

"Sequence," Blair repeated, liking the word for the way it asked less of today and more of tomorrow.

The figure's colors thinned with the failing light. "There will be a cost."

"I know," Blair said.

"No," the figure said, and this time its voice held the firmness of an elder naming weather. "You will be asked to trade belonging for truth. It will feel like exile before it feels like leadership."

Blair's wings trembled. "And if I refuse?"

"Then the hive will keep you," the figure said gently, "and lose itself."

The council announced a forum the next morning. The queen would not take questions, but she would "set direction." A phrase like a ribbon tied over an empty box.

The chamber filled. Honey walls glowed with the theater of order. Overseers lined the platform with their clipboards polished like badges. The queen's voice rolled through the channel, warm as a hearth and just as capable of lulling.

"We celebrate an increase in output," she said. "This proves the wisdom of our checks. We therefore add two more to preserve gains. We will measure our success by the number of attestations completed per shift. Remember: resilience is discipline."

A murmur moved through the room. It was not approval or dissent; it was the noise a body makes when it swallows something that will not digest.

Pip's fingers found Blair's and pressed once. Sera stood, thinner but upright, at their other side. Ilex was a dark shape near the back, arms folded, eyes on the wall more than the throne.

Blair felt the moment as a physical contour—like the lip of a cliff you could step from or retreat behind. The mentor's parable flickered across her mind: shadows measured, combs empty. She imagined the circle with the gap—unfinished by choice.

She lifted her hand.

Not high. Not dramatic. Just enough to say: I am here, and I will speak.

The chamber did not turn toward her. But a few heads did. Enough.

"Define success differently," Blair said—not to the queen, who would not hear, but to the hive that might. Her voice was steady, almost conversational. "Measure nectar, not signatures. Measure walls that do not sag, not placards that warn when they do. Measure rest you can feel, not resilience you must recite."

A small silence widened around her, a clearing made of listening.

An overseer stepped forward, mouth already shaping reprimand. Pip stiffened. Sera reached instinctively for Blair's arm. Ilex, without moving, became a pillar.

Blair did not back away. She did not raise her voice. She simply repeated, "Define success differently."

The reprimand arrived, formal and bland, the kind of scolding that believes tone can smother truth. It listed rules about where and when to speak. It named channels and procedures for questions. It praised the queen's vision and reminded workers to submit proposals through the proper route.

Blair listened until the litany ended, then bowed the smallest possible bow. "Then I will submit a proposal," she said, and because she had already written it with Sable and Ilex—because sequence is a kind of courage—she placed a slate into the overseer's hands.

On it, two columns. Ritual and Essential. Under each, outputs, strain, error. At the bottom, a line Sable had insisted on: *Open circle. Unfinished by choice.*

The overseer took the slate like a bee picks up a thorn. The room exhaled.

After, in the corridor, Pip breathed a laugh that sounded like the first step out of a cage. "You were calm."

"I was deliberate," Blair said.

"Does it matter?"

"It has begun to," Blair replied.

They did not see the queen's eyes narrow in the high chamber, nor the brief exchange of looks between two senior overseers. But they felt something subtle in the hive's hum—a note added, perhaps watchfulness.

That night, the meadow wind shifted. The figure did not appear, and Blair did not panic. She had enough questions to last until morning. She touched the tiny scale hidden in her cell, felt it catch the faint light like a small flame, and let her breathing match the part of the hive that still knew how to sing.

The proposal began its pilgrimage.

First, it went to the Office of Alignment, a room that specialized in arranging words beside other words until they formed a queue. A clerk there admired the neat columns, asked for a cover sheet to describe the cover sheet, then stamped the corner with an emblem of a shield guarding a pen. "Protection of Process," the stamp read, as if process itself were a fragile creature one must keep from the weather.

From Alignment it traveled to Harmonization, where a reviewer suggested replacing the word "strain" with "perceived exertion" and "error" with "variation artifact," both phrases that could live their entire lives without touching a wing. The reviewer also asked whether the "essential checks" had been pre-approved to be called essential. Blair added a note: *checked by wind, approved by outcome.* Sable grinned when he saw it and left it in.

By the time the slate returned from Triage, it wore the fatigue of a traveler who had learned too many ways to say the same thing. The numbers still insisted quietly, but the margins now carried guidance about tone and deference and the importance of not implying that more could sometimes be less.

"It survived," Sable said, peering at the etchings. "Most proposals come home with their meaning shaved off."

"It learned how not to speak," Blair said, "and somehow kept a voice."

Ilex arrived with heat maps showing the east wall's temperature drift, a list of vent adjustments, and a line he refused to delete: *Backlog delays increase structural risk.* He slid the map beside the slate. Even a clerk could see it: where ritual thickened, heat pooled; where honey massed, the wall bent. There was a pattern here that did not care about slogans.

"Now we wait," Ilex said.

"Waiting is a form," Blair replied. "We can fill it with something better."

The illness swelled. It did not announce itself with a fever pitch; it arrived like fog, turning clear lanes gray. Bees who had never missed a shift took an afternoon to lie flat and stare at the honey light as if it were a sky they could not reach. The overseers doubled the drills. They said fatigue fled before the banner of commitment. The banner fluttered; fatigue stayed.

Sera relapsed hard. She blanked mid-pour and tilted, nectar sliding across the comb in a slow sheet that looked like guilt moving. An overseer appeared so quickly it felt rehearsed. He held a form under her nose and asked for a signature to confirm "incident ownership."

"I own nothing," Sera said, her voice thin. "I borrow the strength I have and return it at night."

Blair stepped between them with the precise politeness of a gate that looks decorative until it does not open. "We'll sign in an hour," she said. "After rest."

"This is irregular," the overseer said.

"So are slumps," Blair answered, and guided Sera away.

Pip stayed to clean the spill. She moved with care, lips set, as if tending a wound no one would admit to. When she finished, she pressed her forehead against the comb, just once, the way some bees greet a shrine they've lost faith in but cannot stop visiting.

The council convened a leadership huddle. The phrase fell down through the chambers like an order wrapped in a hug. Ilex was summoned to present his maps. Blair was not invited, but Sable passed a note through the archive's narrow channel: *Your proposal will be discussed without your voice. This is considered efficiency. Prepare what they will not ask.*

Blair returned to the meadow, not to wait for the figure but to practice saying the truth without apology. She spoke to the wind the way one speaks to mirrors when there is no room left for performance.

"Govern outcomes," she said aloud. "Measure nectar, not signatures. Count repairs not drills. Track rest, not slogans. Define success as 'nothing sagged today' and watch how the hive behaves."

A rustle, and then the figure appeared as if it had uncurled from the leaf itself. "You are rehearsing courage," it said.

"I am rehearsing brevity," Blair answered. "Courage will stutter if I let it."

The figure's eyes warmed. "What will you do when they praise your evidence and add more checks?"

"I will run another experiment bigger than they can ignore," Blair said. "But not loud. Not yet."

"Sequence," the figure said, pleased. "A river undermines stone without raising its voice."

Blair thought of Sera, of Pip, of Ilex's maps. "Stone is stubborn," she said.

"Water is patient," the figure replied.

The leadership huddle produced a proclamation, lacquered in certainty: *We will pilot a pilot.* It sounded like an advance and felt like a stall. The plan: create a centralized team to study the possibility of essential checks, two seasons from now, after appropriate attestations. Until then, the hive would add a safeguard: an extra attestation after flight to confirm that the first two attestations were properly attested.

Pip read it, blinked twice, and said, "They studied the shadow and wrote about the sun."

Ilex brought harder news. "I've reached a limit," he said. "The wall needs a structural brace. The kind you bolt into the backbone, the kind that requires someone with a seal to nod. I do not have the seal. I can twirl vents until dawn, and we'll still be one hot day away from honey on the floor."

"Who has the seal?" Blair asked.

Ilex named a senior engineer who had not touched wax in years. "He will want assurance that a brace is aligned with resilience strategy," he said dryly. "He will need proof that preventing a sag is as valuable as responding to one."

"Then we will give him proof that moves," Blair said.

Ilex tilted his head. "Proof that moves?"

Blair's eyes found Pip, who looked back with the quick fear of a bird that still chooses the sky. "A public experiment," Blair said. "We'll run the essential-check route with a small cadre at dawn. We'll invite witnesses who matter: two respected workers, one guard, and—if we can manage it—the engineer with the seal."

"That risks sanction," Ilex warned.

"That risks watching the wall bend until we get a medal for cleaning," Blair replied. "I choose the other risk."

Sable listened, then slid a token across the table: a small disc etched with the open circle. "Carry this. It tells old bees with long memories that what you are doing is not disrespect—it is remembrance."

"What if it tells overseers I am gathering a faction?" Blair asked.

"Then it will teach them a new word," Sable said. "Community."

The dawn chosen for the experiment arrived half a shade before courage. The air held that thin blue patience that makes even loud hearts speak softly. Blair's cadre met at the threshold: Pip; a broad-shouldered worker named Rook known for fairness; a quiet forager called Lami who could recite bloom times the way poets recite lines; and a guard named Vetch whose job made him careful, not cruel. Ilex stood apart, as if trying to not look like an engineer staging a demonstration.

The senior engineer with the seal did not come. He sent an assistant with a notebook and a look that said he had learned politeness as a defense.

"Essential checks only," Blair said. "Wing integrity, latch, storm alert. Ninety seconds. Then fly."

They flew.

The meadow received them the way a balanced room receives silence: with gratitude. The lanes bent clean. The turn at the marker tightened sweetly. Rook returned first, surprised by the confidence in his own arms. Lami arrived with cells so thick the air sang around them. Pip landed and did not tremble.

"Again," Blair said.

They flew again.

When they returned, Ilex had already logged strain and speed. Vetch, who had meant to be neutral, wore the involuntary half-smile of someone who has watched grace argue with paperwork and win. The assistant scribbled something that sounded like doubt learning to try a new shape.

An overseer approached—one they all knew, lacquered voice, tidy rage. "Authorization?" he asked.

"Outcome," Blair said, equal parts answer and invitation.

"This is a violation of procedure."

"This is a demonstration of effectiveness."

He stared at the slate, then at their bodies not shaking, then at the nectar humming in the cells like proof that had learned music. "You cannot present data gathered improperly."

"It is gathered accurately," Ilex said, stepping in. "Your forms are not instruments."

The overseer's mouth tightened. He was not a villain; he was a man trapped inside a definition. "I will report this."

"Report the absence of error," Blair said. "Report the reduction in strain. Report the increase in nectar."

He lifted his stylus, then lowered it, then lifted it again. His training did not include this.

"Come," Vetch said quietly. "See the east wall."

They walked together—Blair, Pip, Ilex, the assistant, the overseer who hated and feared curiosity at the same time. The wall, still bearing yesterday's equilibrium, held steady. The honey line at the seam had dried to a thin amber grin.

"What does this prove?" the overseer asked.

“That time returned to the field does not vanish,” Blair said. “It returns as weight we can hold.” She looked at him, not defiant but insistent. “Define success differently. If we fix the brace, we will not need a parade for our speed.”

The assistant cleared his throat. “The seal-holder will want to see this,” he said, and for the first time his voice held something useful: risk shifting from Blair’s shoulders onto a scale where leaders might finally feel it.

By midday, everyone knew something had happened, though versions disagreed. The council called an emergency review. The queen’s message arrived veiled: *Innovation is encouraged when aligned. Alignment is achieved through channels. Channels protect order. Order protects us all.* Each sentence was true the way well-polished stones are true—hard, smooth, and useless for hunger.

Sera found Blair by the archive. “They will come for you,” she said, not as a warning, but as a promise that she would stand nearby when they did.

“They will come for a story,” Blair answered. “I am only its teller.”

Sable slid the open-circle token back into Blair’s palm, as if to recharge it. “There is one more thing,” he said. “The mentor you see in the meadow—do not bring it proof. Bring it questions.”

“I have more than enough,” Blair said.

“Good,” Sable replied. “Questions are the only cargo that never weighs you down.”

That night the hive hummed with a new note—unease braided with interest. Somewhere in the upper chambers, voices measured consequences. Somewhere in the lower corridors, a worker tried an essential check and then another. The figure did not appear at the meadow’s edge, but Blair felt its absence like approval: she had stepped from student into practice.

She lay awake, the tiny scale by her head catching moonlight, and wondered which would arrive first in the morning: a seal for the brace, or a summons for discipline. The thought frightened her less than it should have. Either would prove the hive had heard her.

And hearing, even before agreeing, is how stone learns the language of water.

The summons came at dawn.

Two guards waited by Blair's cell, wings held stiff, eyes fixed forward. One spoke in the polished cadence reserved for official tasks: "The council requests your presence." The words tasted less like request and more like verdict.

Blair followed, Pip shadowing at a distance until a guard blocked her path. "Not you," he said. Pip's eyes flashed panic, but Blair lifted one hand. *Patience,* the gesture said. *Deliberate, not daring.*

The central chamber loomed larger when approached as a defendant. Honey walls glowed with rehearsed pride. Overseers lined the sides with clipboards ready, not to record truth but to shape it. At the center stood the queen, her presence radiant and heavy, like light that refuses to warm.

"You conducted an unauthorized experiment," the queen began, voice echoing through the chamber. "You endangered process."

Blair bowed slightly, not as submission but as acknowledgment of the stage. "I measured outcomes," she said. "The danger was to ritual, not to life."

A ripple moved through the chamber. Overseers scribbled furiously. The queen's eyes narrowed. "Outcomes are nothing without order. A hive without process is chaos."

"A hive with only process," Blair replied, "is a prison that starves."

Silence pressed down. Even scribes hesitated, their stylus tips hovering above wax.

One overseer broke the tension. "We have her numbers," he said reluctantly. "They show efficiency. But the method was improper."

"Improper data is invalid," another chimed in.

Ilex's voice cut through, calm and deliberate. "Improper according to form, valid according to physics. The wall does not care about attestations. It cares about heat and weight. Outcomes are indifferent to ritual."

The queen turned her gaze on him. "And you support this… deviation?"

"I support braces," Ilex said simply. "And walls that do not sag."

The chamber bristled. No one spoke so plainly in front of the queen. But the silence that followed was not entirely hostile. It carried curiosity, the most dangerous contagion of all.

The queen lifted her wings. "We will deliberate. Until then, the proposal is suspended. The worker known as Blair is placed under observation. If further deviation occurs, sanctions will follow."

Observation—another word polished into threat. It meant eyes at every corner, notes taken on every move. Yet Blair felt no shame as the guards led her out. She felt only the weight of seeds planted.

That evening she walked alone to the meadow, though every instinct warned against it. The figure was waiting, wings shimmering faintly in the dusk.

"You spoke," it said.

"I had to," Blair replied. "They call it deviation. I call it breath."

"And what did they hear?"

"Enough to be afraid," Blair said. "Enough to suspend but not destroy."

The figure studied her. "Fear is a teacher, but a poor leader. What lesson will you leave behind when they remember this day?"

Blair thought. "That outcomes can be seen. That rituals can be weighed. That silence is not the only loyalty."

The figure nodded slowly. "Good. Then you have stepped into the oldest role."

Blair tilted her head. "Which role is that?"

"Mentor," the figure said.

The word startled her. "I am still a student."

"Students who act become teachers, whether they ask to or not," the figure replied. Its wings glowed with a final pulse of color. "Do not wait for my questions. Begin asking your own. Ask until asking becomes contagious."

Blair felt her chest tighten. "Will I see you again?"

The figure's eyes softened. "Perhaps. Or perhaps you no longer need me in this form."

With that, it rose, a slow arc into twilight, dissolving into the horizon like a truth too bright to stare at directly.

The next days blurred into tension. Overseers watched Blair's every step, but watching did not erase whispers. Pip repeated Blair's questions to others, almost shy at first, then steadier: *What do you notice? What story are you telling? What are you willing to risk?* The words spread like quiet pollen, invisible yet persistent.

Sera, fragile but defiant, began measuring her own recovery in outcomes, not rituals. "Today I poured without shaking," she told Pip. "That is resilience. Not the oath I forgot, but the nectar I delivered."

Rook and Lami, the workers who had flown in Blair's experiment, shared their experience with others in guarded tones. "We tried fewer checks," Rook whispered one night. "We returned stronger. We carried more." Their listeners leaned in, the way thirsty bees lean toward water.

Even Vetch, the guard, shifted subtly. He did not look away during inspections, but he no longer looked with suspicion. He looked with thought, and thought is a rebellion overseers cannot chart.

Ilex kept working the vents, patient as water. "The wall will not wait forever," he warned. "Soon we must choose: brace or break."

Blair nodded. "We are already choosing. One question at a time."

The council's decision came quietly, wrapped in neutral words. They approved a single brace for the east wall, "as a temporary safeguard aligned with resilience strategy." They did not credit Blair, or Ilex, or the experiment. They credited "the strength of process to adapt."

But the brace was built. The wall held. Honey did not spill. Workers breathed easier, even if they did not say why.

Pip found Blair that evening, eyes wide. "They gave us the brace. They pretended it was theirs, but they gave it."

Blair smiled faintly. "Let them pretend. Pretending builds walls as well as pride. We will measure what stands."

Sable placed the original slate back in Blair's hands. The numbers had not changed, but they looked different now, like seeds that had sprouted roots. "Keep it," he said. "Truth travels light, but it lasts heavy."

That night Blair lay in her cell, the tiny scale glinting faintly by her side. The hive hummed steady again, but she no longer trusted steady. She had learned that calm could be a pause before collapse, or a breath before transformation.

She closed her eyes and whispered the mentor's last gift: "Ask until asking becomes contagious."

She thought of Pip whispering to others, of Sera redefining resilience, of Ilex holding the wall, of Vetch choosing thought over suspicion. Small questions, spreading. Small cracks in ritual's armor.

She did not know what Chapter 3 of her hive's story would demand. She knew only that the questions had begun to live on their own.

And questions, once alive, are the one thing a hive cannot kill with forms.

3

Cracks in the Comb

The hive woke to a tone sharper than usual, pitched high enough to cut through even the deepest fatigue. Workers stirred in confusion. The overseers claimed it was simply a calibration of the channel, but the sound lingered in the body like an echo of unease.

Blair rose, wings already stiff with the memory of yesterday's summons. She had spoken in the council chamber, and though the queen had suspended her proposal with elegant dismissal, the air inside the hive had not returned to its usual rhythm. Questions hummed just beneath the surface. Questions overseers could not quiet with slogans.

Pip found her near the entrance. "They're watching you more," she whispered.

"I expected that," Blair said.

"They write notes every time you blink."

Blair almost smiled. "Then I'll blink deliberately."

The east wall, newly braced, stood firm. Honey no longer pooled at its seams, though overseers credited the improvement to their "swift oversight." Ilex worked the vents anyway, unwilling to trust a single brace. He murmured calculations under his breath as though speaking directly to physics, bypassing the theater of governance.

Sera returned to partial duties, though her hands still trembled. She poured nectar carefully, each drop a victory. When overseers passed, she stiffened, fearing another infraction. Blair steadied her with a quiet touch.

"You don't need to apologize to honey," Blair said softly.

Sera's lips twitched. "Then to whom do I apologize?"

"To no one," Blair said. "Delivering nectar is apology enough for rest."

Sera exhaled, as if such permission could loosen the tight band around her chest.

DOI: 10.1201/9781003740056-3

By midmorning, the council announced a new initiative. The queen's voice rolled through the hive, smooth and commanding: *We are implementing Operation Fortify. It will ensure that every drop of nectar, every line of comb, every breath of air is documented and aligned. Strength is safety. Safety is survival.*

Workers listened, silent. Overseers scurried to prepare fresh tables, new stamps, and longer queues. Pip muttered under her breath, "Operation Fortify looks a lot like Operation Burden."

Blair's heartbeat faster. *This is how fear grows legs,* she thought. *By naming itself safety.*

Later, in the meadow, the mentor appeared again, shimmering as though it had never left. Blair felt relief tighten into resolve.

"They've launched another initiative," she said. "More forms, more slogans. They call it safety. I call it fear with a banner."

The figure regarded her calmly. "And what do you see beneath the banner?"

"Exhaustion. Distrust. Bees pretending to be strong while collapsing inside."

"And what story are you telling yourself about that exhaustion?"

"That it will kill us before hunger does."

The figure nodded. "Then what must you do?"

Blair hesitated. "Act again. But carefully."

"Carefully," the figure repeated. "Not quietly. Silence does not care—it is complicity."

That evening, Blair gathered her small circle in a shadowed alcove: Pip, Sera, Ilex, and Rook, the fair-minded worker who had flown in the experiment. The hum of the hive muffled their voices, but each spoke with urgency.

"They'll dismiss the brace as coincidence if we don't push further," Ilex said. "One wall does not change culture."

"They're already drowning us in forms," Sera added, voice weary. "I can't survive another initiative like Fortify."

Pip clenched her fists. "Then we show them results. Again. Bigger."

Blair considered. "Not reckless. Deliberate. A demonstration that forces them to see, not just to hear."

Rook tilted his head. "And what if they punish us?"

Blair met his eyes steadily. "Then at least we know the cost of truth. And others will see that cost and ask why it was paid."

Sable appeared unexpectedly, stepping from the archive with a lamp's glow. "Questions are seeds," he said. "But seeds only matter if the ground is ready. You must decide whether your hive is soil or stone."

Blair asked him, "And if it is stone?"

Sable's old eyes glimmered. "Then water will teach it patience."

The illness returned with sharper teeth. Entire flights staggered. Three workers landed short of the meadow and had to be carried back. Overseers labeled them "non-compliant," assigning mandatory resilience drills as punishment. Pip whispered furiously to Blair, "They're punishing collapse with more collapse."

Blair's anger burned hotter than fear. She found Ilex near the vents. "We can't wait for the council's pace. The hive is crumbling under rituals while the walls strain. If we don't act—"

"We will act," Ilex interrupted. "But not just with words. With structures. You gave them numbers. Now give them a vision."

"A vision?" Blair asked.

"Show them what the hive could be," Ilex said. "Not with banners. With outcomes."

That night Blair dreamed of the mentor. In the dream, the figure stood inside the hive itself, walking among overseers unseen. It touched clipboards with one finger, and ink dissolved into clear air. It placed a hand on a wall, and resin patches melted away, replaced by solid wax. It leaned over a worker and whispered, and the worker's wings straightened as though remembering how to fly.

When Blair woke, she still felt the words in her ears: *Do not only dismantle what is false. Build what is true.*

By dawn, her course was clear. She gathered the circle. "We will create a pilot," she said. "Not on paper. In practice. A corridor run with no excess checks, only essentials. We'll track nectar, strain, errors. We'll show that safety is not signatures—it is strength that adapts."

Sera bit her lip. "And if overseers intervene?"

Blair answered with the steadiness of decision. "Then they will have to explain why they punish what works."

Pip grinned, nervous but fierce. "Deliberate, not daring. But maybe daring too."

The morning of the pilot felt heavier than storm air. The corridors hummed with the usual ritual of queues and attestations, but Blair sensed a subtle current beneath it all, as if wings beat slightly out of sync. Pip met her at the threshold, eyes bright with nervous defiance.

"Ilex adjusted the vents last night," Pip whispered. "The east corridor is steady. He says conditions are right."

Sera joined them slowly, shoulders set though her legs trembled. Rook and Lami arrived too, their presence unspoken commitment. Even Vetch, the guard who had once stood in neutral silence, lingered near the entrance as if permission had become curiosity.

Blair's heart pounded, but her voice was even. "Wing check. Latch check. Weather alert. Nothing more. We fly for results, not rituals."

They launched.

The meadow opened before them, clear and golden. Without queues and attestations dragging them, their wings cut clean arcs. Pip laughed mid-flight, the sound sharp and free, startling even herself. Sera carried her load without spill. Rook banked tightly at the marker, strong where fatigue had once bent him.

They returned with nectar that hummed against the cells. Ilex recorded outputs, noting faster circuits, heavier loads, zero errors. The numbers did not need slogans—they sang for themselves.

An overseer appeared, breath clipped, clipboard clutched like a weapon. "Authorization?" he demanded.

"Outcome," Blair said, her calm practiced now.

"This is violation."

"This is evidence." She gestured to the nectar, glistening proof.

The overseer's stylus wavered. "Improper process invalidates data."

Ilex's tone was precise. "Improper process cannot invalidate physics. The wall does not collapse because of missing signatures. It collapses because of strain."

The overseer scribbled furiously, trying to cage reality with ink. Yet Vetch, the guard, spoke quietly beside him: "I saw them. I saw the lanes hold. I saw no error."

The overseer hesitated. Guards were not meant to testify. Yet silence cracked. Truth had witnesses now.

Word spread faster than decrees. Workers whispered of the pilot with hungry awe. "They flew without all the checks," one murmured. "They carried more." Another added, "And no one crashed." A third whispered, "Maybe the rituals are the weakness."

The overseers scrambled to contain it. They issued a bulletin: *Unauthorized deviations undermine resilience. Trust the process. Deviations endanger all.* Yet the bulletin itself felt hollow. Every bee who had seen the pilot knew otherwise.

Pip reported what she overheard in queues. "Some believe us. Some are afraid. But they're talking, Blair. Talking where silence used to live."

Blair smiled faintly. "Questions are living now."

That evening, the mentor appeared, wings shimmering in twilight hues.

"You acted," it said simply.

"We flew," Blair replied. "We proved outcomes matter more than rituals. The overseers deny it, but the workers saw."

"And what do you notice now?"

"That truth spreads faster than slogans. That one small act is heavier than a hundred decrees."

The mentor nodded. "And what story are you telling yourself about this?"

"That change is possible," Blair whispered.

The figure's voice softened. "Careful. Hope is strength, but unchecked, it becomes naiveté. The council will not yield easily. They will strike back harder, not softer. Are you ready for that?"

Blair's chest tightened. "If I am not ready, the hive will never be."

"Then you must prepare your circle," the mentor said. "Teach them to ask not only what is wrong, but what must replace it."

The strike came quicker than expected. The council issued a decree the next morning: *All deviations must be punished by reassignment.* The word reassignment carried the weight of exile. Workers reassigned vanished into menial tasks far from the meadow—wax sorting, ledger copying, shadow patrols. No one returned from reassignment with spirit intact.

The decree named no one, yet all eyes slid toward Blair. Overseers shadowed her steps, their clipboards held tighter. Pip trembled but stayed nearby. Sera whispered, "They will come for you."

Blair steadied her. "Then they must admit what they fear."

Later, in the archive, Sable studied her with his milky eyes. "You stand at the line where symbols become weapons," he said.

"They already are," Blair replied.

"True. But until now they cut only paper. Soon they will try to cut wings."

Blair inhaled. "And if they do?"

"Then you must decide," Sable said. "Do you resist to preserve yourself, or yield to preserve the question?"

The words weighed heavy. She did not answer.

That night, Blair dreamed of the brace on the east wall. In the dream it was not wax or timber but paper—layer upon layer of forms stacked high. When the honey pressed, the paper bent and tore. Overseers stood applauding the collapse, praising the speed of their cleanup. Workers drowned quietly while signatures floated like leaves.

She woke with her chest aching. *We must brace with truth,* she thought, *not paper.*

At dawn she called her circle. "We must expand the pilot. Not just one flight. A cycle. A full day measured by outcomes."

Sera paled. "That will be impossible to hide."

"Exactly," Blair said. "It must be undeniable. They will call it defiance. We will call it survival."

Ilex nodded grimly. "If the data is strong, even the council cannot erase it without cracking their own walls."

Pip clenched her fists. "Deliberate, not daring. But maybe daring too."

Blair looked at each of them. "We choose the risk. We do not let it choose us."

The next morning, their plan would unfold—a full cycle of essential checks only, flown by a cadre large enough to draw notice, steady enough to prove unshakable. Overseers would resist, perhaps punish. But the question was alive now, humming louder than fear: *What if we measured what mattered?*

And once asked, a question is the one thing a hive cannot kill with forms.

They met at first light, when the hive's corridors still smelled like cool wax and unspent breath. The cadre had grown: Blair, Pip, Sera, Rook, Lami, and three more workers whose names traveled softly through the hive—Nyx, who could read the weather by listening to the walls; Bracken, a steady flyer with a carpenter's patience; and Tella, whose laughter usually arrived before her body and stayed after fatigue took the rest. Vetch, the guard, stood again at the threshold, not guarding against them so much as guarding the space for them to pass.

"Essential checks only," Blair said. "No delay. We fly a full cycle."

Ilex had already mapped the air. He moved along the vent levers with the tenderness of someone tuning a sleeping animal—shift here, ease there, a breath out of the corner, a cool tongue of air where heat might pool later. When he looked up, the lines on his face had organized into decision. "You'll have the sky you need," he said. "For now."

They launched.

The meadow opened like a book written in two colors—gold where clover blazed, silver where dew lingered. Their first circuits were tight, shoulders warm, minds elastic. Pip moved with a new economy that made her seem older, a grace earned instead of inherited. Sera flew like a sentence trimmed of qualifiers. Rook and Bracken ran the turn at the marker with a precision that felt like apology for all the times they had apologized to nothing. Tella laughed once, the sound like a coin clink in clear water, and then she got to work.

They returned heavy. Cells thrummed with weight. The first hour's numbers settled on Ilex's slate like birds that meant to stay: faster circuits, lower strain, zero errors. The second hour matched. The third improved practice, it turned out, compounds freedom.

By the fourth hour, their bodies spoke the truth their mouths could only hint at: rituals had been stealing strength they could not spare.

Oversight arrived with an entourage.

Three overseers—polish, posture, precision—advanced on the threshold like a legal document that had learned to walk. Behind them came two clerks, their styluses already wet. A senior officer, one who rarely left the upper chambers, observed from just behind the line, eyes narrowed the way one peers at an insect pinned under glass.

"Cease," the lacquered voice commanded.

Blair hovered just within reach of ground, keeping the conversation horizontal. "On what authority?"

"By decree of Operation Fortify," the officer replied. "All unaligned deviations are to be halted under sanction of reassignment."

"Define alignment," Blair said.

"Alignment is adherence to process."

Blair's wings did not so much as twitch. "Outcomes align a hive to survival. Process aligns a hive to itself. We choose survival."

The officer's mouth hardened. "You choose exile."

Vetch cleared his throat. The sound was not loud, but it belonged to someone whose job was to stand where lines were drawn. "I witnessed zero error," he said. "I witnessed improved output. I witnessed reduced strain."

The officer did not look at him. "Your witnessing is not the instrument."

Ilex stepped forward, slate in hand. "Physics is the instrument."

"Physics is not our jurisdiction," one overseer said.

"It is the wall's," Ilex answered.

Sera, unshaken for the first time in days, placed her cell gently on the table and spoke as if reciting a fact learned by living it. "Resilience is nectar delivered, not oaths recited." She did not look at any of them as she said it; she looked at the honey.

The senior officer gestured. Two guards—neither Vetch—moved to surround Blair. Vetch's eyes flicked to her, apology and resolve sharing the same brief shimmer. Pip stiffened, and Tella's laughter died in her throat like a bird startled in sleep.

"This is your final warning," the lacquered voice said. "Cease the deviation. Return to process."

Blair lifted her hand, palm out, as if receiving a blessing and refusing to mistake it for a blow. "We will continue the cycle," she said. "It is public. It is recorded. You may sanction afterward. But you will not stop us from finishing what every worker here has seen: safety gained, not promised."

The senior officer hesitated—not at the words, but at the crowd that had gathered without gathering. Workers had stopped moving their feet, which is the body's way of voting. Over in the shadows, Sable stood with his lamp held high enough to be mistaken for ceremony. Rook inhaled and squared his shoulders; Bracken's carpenter patience converted into structure; Lami began quietly counting blooms as if to anchor the world in a number that would hold.

"Fly," Blair said, and they did.

The next hours happened inside two worlds at once—the cool, precise world of outcome and the heated, brittle world of procedure. In outcome-world, the cadre ran cycles that grew not wild but exact, a discipline of removal. In procedure-world, forms gestated, reprimands assembled themselves like winter clouds, and the phrase *under observation* gathered weight until it could be used as a cudgel.

Mid-cycle, a worker from another lane clipped a thorn and tumbled, skidding to a stop. The cadre diverted. Pip reached her first, Sera second. No one asked for signatures. They checked wing integrity, rinsed the scrape with clean dew, walked her to shade, and waited until her eyes steadied.

The senior officer watched, pen hovering over reprimand. "Unauthorized medical deviation," he murmured.

"Effective care," Ilex said.

The worker stood, tested a wing, and smiled the small smile of someone who knows they have not been abandoned to process. She returned to her lane, slower but sure.

The officer did not write.

By late afternoon, resistance shifted strategies. If sanction could not stop them mid-flight without drawing blood, the council would move consequence to after the finish line. Word came down the corridor like cooled lava: *Reassignment papers prepared for Blair and any known associates. Effective dusk.*

Pip heard it first. "They will end us," she whispered.

"They will end our roles," Blair said. "They cannot end what we made visible."

"Visibility will not feed us," Sera answered, steady even in fear.

"No," Blair said. "But it will starve their story."

Vetch leaned in, voice a private corridor. "They plan to separate you from the workers before shift end. If you intend to speak, speak before they take the room."

Speak—about what? Complaint is a sermon no one remembers. Blair closed her eyes and saw the open circle token, the gap that meant unfinished by choice. She opened them and climbed onto a low rise of comb near the threshold. Not high. Enough.

"Hive," she said—not loud, but the word touched a nerve and the chamber hushed. "Define success differently."

It was not new, but it had grown teeth since the first time. She did not sermonize. She named outcomes: "Walls that do not sag. Nectar delivered without tremor. Wings that do not fail from waiting. A ledger measured in honey, not in signatures."

She pointed to the wall, to Sera's still hands, to the slate where Ilex had stopped writing only because numbers without end look like faith.

"We will be reassigned," she said, simple as weather. "But the wall will remember the brace. Your bodies will remember today's absence of ache. The meadow will remember your speed."

Silence held. The senior officer's eyes narrowed, but an odd expression—something between effort and respect—touched the corner of his mouth. "Finish your cycle," he said, and for once his tone sounded like a person and not a policy.

They finished.

Dusk bled into the corridors. The reassignment papers arrived folded like little coffins. A clerk with careful hands held them out to Blair, Pip, Sera, Ilex, Rook, Bracken, Lami, Tella, and Vetch. Vetch raised his eyebrows at the inclusion of his name, then half-smiled as if a private decision had just become public.

Sable stepped forward, lamp steady. "If we are to assign anything," he said, "assign authorship correctly." He placed an archive tablet on the table. On it, two columns: Ritual and Essential. Outputs. Strain. Error. A third column added that day in Sable's clear hand: Care—instances of aid rendered without ritual delay. The numbers stood without posture.

The clerk swallowed. "I… am to collect signatures."

Sable nodded to the slate. "Then sign what happened."

The clerk hesitated, then wrote his name in the margin—small, but in ink. The senior officer said nothing.

They walked together toward the reassignment wing, a procession dignified by the fact that it was unnecessary. Workers lined the corridor, not in protest but in presence. Some touched their foreheads to the comb. Some lifted a hand the way a body salutes without uniforms. Sera's steps did not falter. Pip's chin did not drop. Ilex looked at the vents as if committing their angles to memory.

Halfway there, the hum changed. It moved through the hive like a chord cut clean. The queen's voice entered the channel—measured, ceremonial. *Effective immediately, Operation Fortify is paused pending review. Essential checks pilot authorized in limited corridors under supervision. The council affirms that resilience includes prevention and care.*

The procession stopped without needing to be told. The senior officer exhaled, then folded the papers without handing them over. Vetch took his copy and tore it once, neatly, like a ribbon no longer needed at the opening of a room already in use.

Pip's eyes filled. "Did we win?" she whispered.

Blair shook her head gently. "We began."

Sera turned her palms upward as if to catch a fall that didn't come. "Then we rest," she said, "and fly again."

The senior officer approached Blair. Up close, he looked less lacquered. "History will not record your name," he said, not unkindly. "It will record a committee's."

Blair smiled, not unkindly either. "History can have the committee," she said. "Give the hive the outcomes."

He nodded once, an engineer's nod borrowed for an evening. "Tomorrow, supervised. The day after, measured. After that... we will see."

"We will ask," Blair replied.

She felt, not saw, a flicker at the meadow's edge through the open threshold—color that did not belong to bees, patience given wings. The mentor did not enter. It hovered and turned away, as if escorting them not into safety, but into competence.

Night came. The hive hummed a steadier tone, the kind that can hold grief and momentum at once. In her cell, Blair placed the tiny scale beside the open-circle token. She did not pray. She did not plan. She let the questions breathe in the dark like living things.

And somewhere above, where the honey walls met the cool of the vents, the brace held without ceremony. The ledger measured nectar. The forms would, for a while, learn to say less.

The morning after the queen's pause order, the hive felt like a room after thunder—air rinsed, nerves alert. Overseers arrived early to erect the scaffolding of "supervision." They placed observation rails along the east corridor, positioned two clerks at the threshold, and hung a placard the size of a small door: *Essential Checks Pilot—Authorized.* The word authorized worked like balm for some, like a leash for others.

Blair gathered the cadre beneath the sign. Pip traced a finger along the edge of the placard as if to test whether the permission would hold. Sera flexed her hands, gaze steady, tremor diminished but not gone. Ilex had slept little; he adjusted vents with the meticulousness of someone asked to rescue their own argument.

The senior officer—less lacquered up close—stood with a small cohort. "We observe," he said. "We do not interfere. We reserve the right to end the pilot if risk increases."

Blair nodded. "Define risk."

"Deviation from safety," he said.

"Define safety," Blair replied.

The corner of his mouth flicked. "Walls that do not sag. Bees that do not fall. Honey that does not waste."

"Then we agree," Blair said, and for the first time the word we did not feel like a dare.

They launched.

The supervised corridors changed the act without changing the fact. Essential checks—wing integrity, latch, weather alert—took a sliver of a minute. The lanes accepted them with the quiet welcome of a structure finally used as intended. Observers scribbled; clerks tallied; Ilex listened for heat and found balance where panic had lived. Vetch ranged the edges to keep curious onlookers clear without turning curiosity into crime.

By the second hour, the numbers held. By the third, they improved. In the fifth, something subtle happened: a worker outside the cadre mirrored the cadence—no cue, only recognition. She moved through the threshold with a calm that looked like learned memory. The clerk opened his mouth to object, then closed it. The pilot, it seemed, was contagious.

The council's countermovement arrived not as a reprimand but as a ribbon. They sent down a team called *Enablement*—polite, articulate bees with fresh wax on their wings and phrases that made control sound like care.

"We love what you're doing," their lead cooed. "We want to scale it responsibly. We'll need a governance layer, an oversight framework, a change committee, and a communication plan. We'll also need to standardize the definition of 'essential' so it can be endorsed by our Assurance Board."

Pip stared at them as if they had offered to pave the meadow.

"Your words are very smooth," Sera said, weary rather than unkind. "Do they have edges where we can hold them?"

The Enablement lead smiled brilliantly. "Edges can cut. We prefer rounded language."

"Rounded language rolls downhill," Ilex murmured, too low for them to hear.

Blair stepped forward. "You may standardize after you understand. The pilot will run a full cycle before you name committees. Governance after evidence, not instead of it."

"Of course," the lead said, as if this had been their idea all along. "We'll schedule a listening session. And a listening session about the listening session."

When they left, Tella made a soft cough that passed for laughter. "They want to make a meadow out of meeting rooms."

"Let them meet," Blair said. "We will measure."

At midday, the mentor appeared at the meadow's edge, neither nearer nor farther than usual. Blair flew out alone, heart thudding with the relief of a familiar horizon.

"They paused the operation," Blair said. "They authorized the pilot. Now they want to own it with rounded words."

"And what do you notice?" the figure asked.

"That co-optation is friendlier than repression," Blair said. "It stains slower."

The figure's wings shimmered, amused. "Then ask a sharper question: what cannot be co-opted?"

Blair thought. "Outcomes," she said finally. "And care."

"Why care?" the figure pressed.

"Because care happens in real time," Blair answered. "It's not transportable as a slogan. You either tend the fallen or you don't. The comb knows."

The figure inclined its head. "Good. Hold care at the center. Make it your metric in public. Numbers open the door. Care keeps the door from being replaced with a sign."

"What about you?" Blair asked suddenly, the question rising without permission. "What are you? Who are you to me?"

The figure was quiet long enough for the wind to speak first. "I am a habit with a face," it said at last. "I am the part of your hive that did not die when fear grew tall. Call me mentor if it helps you listen. Call me echo if it helps you speak."

"Will you stay?" Blair asked.

"I will appear when questions need shape," the figure said. "I will recede when questions have legs."

It lifted off, a slow arc into the brighter slice of sky, then settled back like a promise to remain near enough to be missed.

Afternoon brought the council's first "listening session." They staged it in the central chamber, with rugs that softened the honey floor and cushions that made it seem safe to tell the truth. The queen did not attend; her absence was billed as faith in the process.

Workers came because they were tired. Enablement arranged chairs in a circle and asked for "reflections." The first few were tender in the way confessions are when bruises are still new. A worker spoke of waiting in queues until her focus thinned; another described the shame of signing a form with a tremor he pretended was cold.

Sera rose and spoke simply: "Resilience is nectar delivered, not oaths recited." The words landed like a low chime. No one clapped, but several took a breath that was not small.

Blair kept her contributions short: "We measured. Output up. Strain down. Error zero. Care present." She let the four sentences sit like four walls of a room that would stand without decoration.

An overseer in the back—young, eyes too earnest to be lacquered—raised a hand. "If this is true," he said, "why did we not see it before?"

Sable, from the doorway, answered without entering. "Because you measured the shadow at noon and called it courage."

The young overseer flushed, not from shame but recognition. He wrote something on his clipboard and circled it twice. Blair did not know what he had circled, but she knew it mattered to him.

By the final hours of the cycle, the pilot had run long enough to become boring—success's favorite disguise. Boredom was a good sign. It meant the method held without ceremony. The senior officer watched with a stillness that might have been skepticism on its lunch break. Twice he leaned to speak and did not.

Ilex brought Blair a last slate. "Outputs sustained. Strain remains collapsed. We logged three instances of care rendered without ritual delay." He hesitated. "One more thing."

He led Blair to the east wall. The brace sat without posture, simply doing what braces do. Above it, someone had scraped a small open circle into the wax. The symbol looked older than the wall itself.

"Not me," Ilex said.

"Not me," Blair replied.

Sable's lamp flickered near the corner. He did not claim authorship.

Pip touched the mark with an almost superstitious caution. "Unfinished by choice," she whispered. "Maybe that's what we all are."

"Good," Blair said. "Finish only what should not change."

At dusk, Enablement returned with a draft communiqué: *The council celebrates the success of the Essential Checks Pilot. Next steps include establishing the Resilient Essentials Committee (REC), with subcommittees on Assurance, Adoption, and Storytelling. We will develop a Center of Excellence to ensure consistency, build templates, and monitor adherence to the essential framework.*

Tella made her cough-laugh again. "They built a temple to a door."

Blair read the draft carefully. There were no lies in it—only replacements. She handed it back. "Replace 'monitor adherence' with 'monitor outcomes.' Replace 'storytelling' with 'care reporting.' Keep the committees if you must. But put the words we can hold."

The lead blinked, surprised by the precision. "We can… consider that."

"Consider is a hallway," Sera said. "Pick a room."

To his credit, the lead scratched out *adherence* and wrote *outcomes* with a small frown that looked like someone trying on a new shoe. "We'll bring this to the board."

"Bring the numbers," Ilex said. "Boards like wood and data."

That night, Blair sat with Pip on the threshold, their feet dangling over the dark. The meadow breathed the kind of quiet that isn't empty; it's full of things that have stopped pretending to be louder than they are.

"I was afraid the pause would be the end," Pip confessed. "Like a lullaby to put us back to sleep."

"Maybe it was meant to be," Blair said. "But sleep didn't fit anymore."

Pip leaned her head briefly against Blair's shoulder, a gesture free of rank. "Do you think the queen knows?" she asked.

"She knows something," Blair answered. "Whether she knows the right thing is a different question."

"What's the right thing?"

Blair looked at the small open circle on the wall, catching the moon. "To leave some things unfinished on purpose."

The hum of the hive slid into a key that felt sustainable. Not triumphant—triumph is brittle—but durable, the kind a body can carry. Somewhere in the archive, Sable filed a new slate under a symbol that meant *beginning we intend to keep beginning.* Somewhere above, the brace held.

And just at the edge of sight, a flicker of impossible color hovered and then was gone, like a habit choosing not to be needed.

The communiqué returned from Enablement with edits—some good, some slippery. *Monitor outcomes* had survived. *Care reporting* had been moved to a footnote, as if tenderness were a liability. The new headline read: *Council Champions Essential Checks.* History, it seemed, had chosen its author.

Blair read the draft with Pip and Sera in the archive's quiet. Sable's lamp made a patient circle of light.

"They will tell it as if they pulled us," Pip said.

Sera's mouth tilted. "Let them. We needed the pull, even if we provided the rope."

Sable tapped the margin where a tidy sentence declared *success validated by governance.* "Remember," he murmured, "governance can validate, but it must not claim."

"How do we keep them from claiming?" Pip asked.

"We keep making the next thing true," Blair said. "Truth that continues is hard to steal."

Morning brought the first oversight walk-through from the new Resilient Essentials Committee—three members in crisp sashes, the senior officer walking beside them, less lacquered with each passing day. They asked good questions, or at least better ones.

"What is the failure mode if essential checks miss a fault?" one said to Ilex.

"Same as now," Ilex answered, "except it will happen less because we're not exhausting bees before they fly."

A second member stood with Sera and watched her pour. "How do you measure care?"

Sera didn't hesitate. "By the number of times we helped without waiting for permission," she said. "By the number of workers who returned to the meadow because we didn't let them fall alone."

The third watched Pip's preflight and frowned slightly. "You seem calm," she said, as if calm were suspicious.

"I know what matters," Pip replied. "Knowing is lighter than pretending."

The senior officer took notes. He did not interrupt. At one point he looked up at Blair and gave a very small nod, a gesture of someone learning to move a piece of furniture inside himself.

By midday, Enablement staged a "success forum," this one with banners designed in a new palette that suggested modesty. Blair stood near the back. She had no wish to stand on a stage that would try to use her as proof and then file her under *resolved.* Instead, she listened.

The committee presented the data: outputs up, strain down, errors at zero across the pilot lanes. They presented three stories of care, anonymized but intact: a tumble tended, a tremor steadied, a worker walked back from panic by a colleague who chose presence over procedure. The room did not applaud; it exhaled. The difference mattered.

When questions opened, a worker from a distant corridor stood. "If this is now 'authorized,'" she asked, "what will keep you from adding steps back in once we are quiet?"

It was a better question than most speeches. The room shifted toward the answer like a body leaning into wind.

The senior officer surprised them. "Outcomes," he said. "We will measure walls that do not sag. We will measure nectar that does not spill. We will measure days when workers do not fall because they are forced to stand still in queues." He paused. "We will measure care rendered without permission."

Enablement's lead blinked but did not argue. The committee wrote *care* in a box as if testing whether the word could live on a diagram. Sable caught Blair's eye and smiled around the edges, the way old bees smile when a page turns.

That evening, the mentor met Blair at the meadow's edge. The light felt level, neither forgiving nor severe.

"They began to use your words," the figure observed.

"They began to use our outcomes," Blair corrected. "Words went along for the ride."

"And what do you notice now?"

"That co-optation can be converted into alignment—if we keep evidence moving."

"And your story?"

Blair considered. “That leadership is not a person. It’s a posture. Today, some who wore posture learned to inhabit it.”

The figure’s wings flickered, pleased. “Then be careful of a subtler trap.”

“What trap?”

“Becoming necessary,” it said. “If the hive cannot proceed without you, you have not led—you have replaced ritual with yourself.”

Blair let the warning settle. “So, I should make myself smaller?”

“Make the questions larger,” the figure said. “Teach others to ask them before you arrive.”

She thought of Pip speaking to workers in corridors, of Sera answering a committee member as if she were already on the committee, of Ilex demonstrating physics to policy without apology. The questions had legs now. Good.

“Will you come when I call?” she asked.

“I come when questions need shape,” the figure repeated gently. “Soon, you will be the shape.”

It lifted, not departing so much as dispersing into a wind that had learned to hold meaning.

The next week salted the gains with grit. In one lane, a supervisor attempted to “enhance” essentials by adding a fresh attestation—just one, he said, hardly a burden. Output dipped; strain rose. The numbers told the story like a friend refusing to lie. The committee removed the extra step with a memo that was shorter than usual. No banners, no victory songs. Just subtraction.

Another corridor claimed they were “too unique” for essentials and lobbied for exemption. They presented a special-case slide deck. Ilex arrived with heat maps and quiet physics, laying their uniqueness next to reality until the gap looked like posture rather than necessity. They joined the pilot.

Enablement drafted a “Center of Excellence” charter. Blair and Sera edited it together, replacing verbs that meant “manage” with verbs that meant “learn,” swapping *adherence reviews* for *outcome reviews,* and adding a line-item Sable insisted on: *Archive open questions alongside closed decisions.* The charter felt lighter when it was done, a plan that left gaps on purpose.

Pip started a small circle for new flyers who had never known the before-times. She taught them the three essentials and then taught them a fourth: ask. "If something doesn't make sense," she told them, "Ask what it's for. If no one can answer without a slogan, fly the smallest safe experiment and bring back the truth."

"Is that allowed?" a young one whispered.

"It is now," Pip said, and realized she believed it.

The queen called for a private audience.

Blair entered a chamber whose walls were less ornate than legend suggested. The queen stood by a window cut to the meadow—a generous view that few were given. The air carried a steadier tone, as if this room had learned to absorb drama.

"You have been busy," the queen said, not unkindly.

"I have asked," Blair answered. "Others answered."

The queen studied her. "Do you think I did not want outcomes?"

"I think you wanted safety," Blair said, careful, "and that fear told you safety looks like signatures."

The queen did not flinch. "Fear speaks convincingly when one sits where I sit."

"Then move the chair," Blair said, and surprised herself with the clean audacity of it.

A corner of the queen's mouth lifted. "The chair is the chair." She turned back to the window. "This hive is older than both of us. It tolerates experiments when the honey holds. It punishes them when the honey spills. You have given us a way to carry more without spilling. You have my attention."

"Attention is not endorsement," Blair said.

"It is the only coin that spends here," the queen replied. "Spend it wisely."

Blair bowed—not low, but real—and left with the odd sensation of having been neither blessed nor threatened, only invited to continue.

The chapter did not end with a banner. It ended with a maintenance schedule and a small ceremony that wasn't a ceremony: the senior officer, Ilex, Sera, Pip, and two engineers tightening the brace by a quarter turn while a clerk took notes that were useful instead of tidy. Above them, the small open circle caught dusk and made a soft moon for whoever needed it later.

Blair stood back, letting others give the instructions she could have given. Rook and Bracken had drafted a one-page "how to run essentials" guide with spaces for local variation. Lami kept the bloom calendar current and pinned where everyone could see it. Vetch instituted a guard practice: intervene less, observe more, step in only when care needed a corridor.

Sable filed a final slate for the season: outcomes, strain, errors, care, decisions taken, questions kept open. He stamped it with a mark Blair hadn't seen before—two circles, not touching, with a slender line between. "Bridge," he said when she asked. "For when gaps refuse to be closed and must be crossed."

Night arrived clean. The hive hummed in a key that felt earned. Blair sat on the threshold with Pip. They shared honey without talking, a proof that does not require minutes.

"What's next?" Pip asked at last.

"Not more," Blair said. "Deeper." She nodded toward the darker corridors, where rituals still lived with sharper teeth. "Audit the places we were afraid to look. Ask in rooms that echo differently. Brace what bends. Retire what only looks like strength."

"And the mentor?" Pip asked.

Blair glanced at the meadow. Color flickered at the edge of sight and did not come closer. "Questions are walking now," she said. "It will keep up."

They rose. Tomorrow would be the season's last flight before the weather turned. After that, harder work—the kind done with diagrams and schedules, with teaching and refusing to let teaching turn into ceremony.

At her cell, Blair placed the open-circle token beside the tiny scale and, for the first time, did not wonder whether she would be reassigned in the morning. The brace held. The ledger measured nectar. The committees, for now, measured outcomes. The questions had found many mouths.

And somewhere beyond the meadow, something larger than a hive turned in its sleep, as if waking would be required soon.

4

The Council's Mirror

The hive hummed with an unfamiliar steadiness. For days, the east wall had held without sag, the brace firm, the vents breathing in rhythm with the comb. The overseers had declared the Essential Checks Pilot a success, and for once their announcement was not immediately met with mutters or lowered wings. There was relief in the corridors, even a flicker of pride.

Yet Blair could not settle. The hum sounded too smooth, like a tune rehearsed rather than lived. She caught herself listening harder, straining for the stutter that usually betrayed reality. The absence of imperfection felt more like silence than peace.

Pip, however, glowed with energy. She darted between flights, reminding new workers of the three essential checks. "Latch, wings, weather," she recited like a rhyme, and the youngest repeated after her as if it had always been so. Her pride was genuine, her joy a balm.

Sera, though still weary, poured with steadier hands. "I can hold again," she told Blair one evening, voice fragile but resolute. "Not forever, but enough."

Ilex logged the outputs daily, filling slates with numbers that left little room for doubt. He showed Blair one: *output up 23 percent, strain down 31 percent, errors zero across five corridors.*

"Hard to argue with," he said.

Blair nodded, but unease threaded her. "When has the council ever failed to argue with reality?"

The announcement came on the third morning. The queen's voice filled the hive with the practiced warmth of ceremony:

> *"We begin a new season of listening. We will reflect worker voices back into governance. We name this Operation Mirror."*

The words slid across wax like polish. Overseers applauded. Workers tilted their heads, uncertain whether to feel seen or staged.

DOI: 10.1201/9781003740056-4

Within hours, posters appeared on honey walls: *Your Voice, Our Strength.* A new cadre of "worker representatives" was appointed bees selected not from the meadow's-tired lanes but from tidy records of compliance. They smiled with nervous pride, already repeating the council's slogans as if they had always believed them.

Meetings were scheduled in every corridor. "Listening sessions," they were called. Chairs arranged in circles, overseers at the edges pretending not to guide the discussion. Questions were permitted, but answers were read from tablets prepared in advance.

"They are using our words," Pip whispered to Blair after one such session. "They said outcomes, care, resilience. Exactly like us. But it felt..." She trailed off.

"Hollow," Blair finished. "Like honey drained of nectar."

The circle gathered in the archive, where Sable's lamp burned steadier than any council decree. Sera sat with her hands folded, Ilex leaned against a shelf, Pip paced, and Rook listened quietly as if weighing timber before cutting.

"They've stolen our language," Pip said bitterly. "Every phrase we fought for, now they chant it like slogans."

"Better stolen than silenced," Sera murmured. "If the words spread, does it matter whose mouth carries them?"

"It matters," Ilex said. "If words mean everything, they mean nothing. We need the wall braced, not the banner raised."

Blair rubbed her temple. "They are turning questions into mirrors. The workers speak, and the council reflects back only what flatters them. Reflection is not seeing."

Sable looked up from his lamp. "Mirrors bend truth when framed too tightly. Even honest faces look strange."

"So, what do we do?" Pip demanded. "Fight the words they've stolen?"

"No," Blair said softly. "We must show outcomes they cannot mimic. Something beyond reflection."

That night Blair flew to the meadow, wings heavy with thought. The mentor appeared before her, shimmering with dusk's colors.

"They've taken our language," she said. "They repeat outcomes, care, resilience—but only as ceremony. How do we fight when truth wears their costume?"

The figure studied her. "Do you fight to defeat the system, or to renew it? And what is the difference?"

Blair faltered. Destroying the hive had never been her aim. Renewal was her hope, but renewal felt false if it came clothed in lies.

The mentor's wings pulsed. "When mirrors lie, even truth looks bent. You must teach them to see without reflection."

Blair frowned. "How?"

"By building something that casts no shadow," the figure said. "A practice so plain it cannot be disguised. Care that happens in the moment. Outcomes so clear no mirror can distort them."

Blair whispered the word as if tasting it for the first time: "Care."

The figure leaned closer. "Governance will always try to measure what is easiest. Teach them that what matters most cannot be reduced to slogans. Make care your proof. Make it your ledger."

Then it dissolved into twilight, leaving Blair with nothing but the steady insistence of its question: *What cannot be co-opted?*

The next day, the first signs of strain returned. Not structural—cultural. Workers grew restless in the listening sessions, realizing their words traveled only in circles. Some left midway. Others repeated questions overseers ignored, voices louder each time.

The illness, never gone, sharpened its grip. Two workers collapsed mid-flight, carried back pale and ashamed. Overseers blamed "transition fatigue," insisting resilience drills would restore them. But the drills broke more than they fixed.

Sera pressed her lips together. "They call it fatigue from reform. I call it exhaustion from pretending."

Ilex scowled over his heat maps. "We fixed the brace, but the hive is sick in its marrow. Data won't matter if collapse comes from the body, not the walls."

Pip clenched her fists. "Then we show them. Again. Another demonstration. Bigger this time. Not just essential checks—essential care."

Blair's heart lifted at the word. She thought of the mentor's warning. *Care cannot be co-opted.* Perhaps Pip had spoken the next step aloud.

They met in the archive at dusk, the light thin as old wax. Sable's lamp drew a modest circle; outside it, shadows arranged themselves like listeners who had chosen not to speak.

"We need something they can't polish," Pip said, pacing. "Something that doesn't look good on a poster."

"Posters aren't the problem," Sera murmured. "The problem is when posters substitute for proof."

Ilex spread two slates on the table: outputs and strain from pilot corridors; a scatter of incidents labeled *care given* with brief marks—no names, only moments: *wing rinse, dew; tremor steadied; panic walked down.* "These entries aren't formal," he said. "But the pattern is real. Where care happens in the moment, strain collapses. Where care is delayed by ritual, error blooms."

Rook leaned in. "Then measure care."

"We are," Ilex said, tapping the small marks. "But we need a demonstration they cannot deny. Not an argument. A sight. Something that makes denial look expensive."

Blair felt the mentor's question surface: *What cannot be co-opted?* "Care," she said aloud. "Not as a value, as a practice."

Sable nodded slowly. "If you must put care in a ledger, let the ink be speed and steadiness: how fast did we tend, how gently did we return, how soon did the worker fly again."

"And where rituals prevented it," Sera added, "mark the delay as a wound."

Pip's eyes brightened. "A comparison flight. Two corridors. One under Mirror's ceremonies—listening sessions, extra attestations. One under essentials plus on-the-spot care. We invite witnesses. We don't argue outcomes. We let them land against their owners."

"And we brace for consequences," Ilex said.

Blair looked around the circle. "Deliberate, not daring," she said—then allowed herself the smallest smile. "And a little daring."

Operation Mirror thickened overnight. Worker representatives received sashes; there were practice runs for the "reflect and affirm" protocol—questions asked, answers mirrored, gratitude expressed, nothing changed. The new slogan unfurled across honey walls: *See Ourselves to Save Ourselves.*

"They are mistaking reflection for vision," Rook said, almost gently, as if correcting a child.

The council announced a showcase for the end of the week: *Mirror in Action.* It would feature testimonies, metrics, and a panel. The queen would attend. The words moved through the hive like perfume—pleasant, a little heavy, masking something older.

"Good," Blair said. "We'll hold our comparison flight the morning of the showcase. If they prefer mirrors, we'll give them a window."

Pip laughed—quick, sharp, the sound of fear agreeing to be useful.

The illness surged as if offended by slogans. A veteran forager named Min fell out of rhythm, flaring mid-turn and scraping a wing. She froze at the threshold, ashamed. A clerk hurried toward her with a form; an overseer called for a resilience recitation.

"Stop," Sera said, voice flat with clarity. "Wing first."

Pip fetched dew. Ilex guided Min to shade, checking the joint with the patience he used on vents. Blair stood between Min and the form as if her body were a modest wall. No one shouted. No memo announced a new policy. Care entered the scene the way a hand enters water.

Min's breath slowed. Within minutes she flexed and nodded. "I can go again," she said, surprised at her own voice.

The clerk, to his credit, lowered the form. "Note: resolved without escalation," he wrote—then, after a moment, added, "care given."

He glanced up at Blair, as if asking whether he had used the right word. She did not correct him.

That night, the mentor did not appear. Blair did not need it to. She walked the edge of the meadow and practiced the speech she would not give: no indictments, no grand metaphors. She would point, like a carpenter teaching a novice to see a bow in a board.

"Here," she whispered to the grass. "Ritual delays care. Outcomes suffer. Here: essentials plus care. Outcomes hold." She could feel the words shrinking, condensing, losing fat and gaining bone. Good. The hive had eaten enough sugar.

When she returned, Sable waited at the threshold with an old token: not the open circle this time, but two parallel lines joined by small rungs. "Ladder," he said. "For climbing out of holes we dig with our habits. Keep it in your pocket; do not show it. Some symbols work best in the hand."

Blair slid it under her band, where the metal warmed against her.

Dawn of the comparison flight arrived with a sky so clean it looked invented. Two corridors marked quietly: Mirror Lane and Meadow Lane. In Mirror Lane, everything arranged for optics—placards, representatives with sashes, a clerk assigned to "capture sentiment." In Meadow Lane, almost nothing—only the three essentials and an agreed practice: any worker who faltered would be tended immediately by the nearest capable bee.

Witnesses arrived: Vetch as guard; the young overseer with earnest eyes; two engineers; a worker from a distant corridor who'd written letters with real questions; and, unexpectedly, the senior officer himself, plain sash, clipboard held like a tool instead of a shield.

Blair briefed them once. "Observe time to tend. Observe time to return. Observe outputs, strain, and spills."

The young overseer frowned. "And if the day is unusually calm?"

"Then the numbers will be uninteresting," Blair said. "Boredom is success."

They launched.

In Mirror Lane, the first fault came slow—a hesitance mid-turn from a worker rehearsing the "reflect and affirm" answers she would offer at the showcase. She clipped a stem, steadied, then paused at the threshold, ashamed. A representative moved toward her with a practiced smile; an overseer invited a debrief. The clerk lifted his stylus, ready for sentiment.

"Wing," the worker whispered.

"After we record," the representative said gently.

The delay was brief by ritual standards—two minutes only. But two minutes are heavy when pain can be rinsed in ten seconds. When care finally arrived, the wing was already swelling; the second circuit delivered light. The clerk recorded satisfaction with the listening experience.

In Meadow Lane, the first fault was faster—a crosswind nudged a young flyer. Pip caught her elbow mid-air, two bodies making a third balance. Sera walked her to shade; Ilex tilted the dew vial without a word. The worker returned within the span of a small story. The second circuit delivered heavy. There was no form.

By the third hour, differences compiled themselves. Mirror Lane tallied three delays for "protocol;" Meadow Lane tallied four instances of care rendered immediately and zero spills. Outputs diverged like paths—one trimmed by cautionary ceremony, the other widened by presence.

Vetch spoke only once, to the senior officer: "I can guard either lane. Only one needs guarding."

The senior officer nodded without writing.

Midday brought wind. Not dramatic—just the kind that tests whether practices are cosmetic or structural. Mirror Lane held, but poorly; the extra attestations made queues brittle. A worker grew dizzy while waiting; sentiment was captured, care delayed. Meadow Lane flexed; when two bees faltered in opposite corners, Tella and Rook split the difference with the ease of rehearsed attention.

The young overseer approached Blair, face working. "I was told Mirror would protect," he said. "But it protects the mirror."

"It reflects activity," Blair said. "Not truth."

He looked toward the engineers. "We need to record the *care index* you spoke of—time to tend, time to return."

Ilex had already etched columns: *tend time, return time, output delta.* He added a small mark Sable suggested: a ladder where care had pulled someone back quickly. The slate began to look like a plan rather than a verdict.

Toward late afternoon, a real test arrived. A gust, a swirl, two near collisions. In Mirror Lane, the representative raised a hand for calm; the clerk prepared a statement; the overseer called for a reflection pause. Two minutes passed. One worker sat down and did not rise for another five.

In Meadow Lane, Bracken shifted lanes to block wind for a second; Pip and Sera executed a practiced exchange—dew, wing, walk, breathe. The young flyer who had wobbled in the morning returned with surprising speed, and on her next turn, she laughed once, short and real, the sound you make when a fear shrinks to fit the hand that's holding it.

The senior officer lowered his clipboard. "I don't need any more writing," he said, not to anyone and to everyone.

"Then look," Blair said quietly.

He did.

They ended the comparison on time, not to dramatize but to settle. Numbers stood, tidy and stubborn: Meadow Lane outran Mirror by measures no mirror could improve—tend times halved, returns doubled, output up, spills nil. The earnest overseer wrote one line on his slate and underlined it twice: *Care is governance in time.*

Pip, exhilarated and spent, leaned against the threshold. "They can polish language," she panted, "but they can't polish speed."

Sera wiped her hands, steady. "They can edition truth, but they cannot own it."

Ilex packed the slates like instruments after a performance. "We bring these to the showcase," he said. "Let them hold the weight in their hands."

Sable blew out his lamp and relit it, a small ritual no one tried to co-opt. "Mirrors are useful," he said. "But only when they hang in rooms with windows."

Blair tucked the ladder token back under her band. The window would open in the morning. The queen would sit. The slogans would arrive with bows. But the room would contain something heavier than words.

And heavy things, properly placed, reframe a house.

The showcase opened with polished restraint. Rugs softened the honey floor; chairs formed a precise horseshoe facing a low dais. The placard above the dais read *Mirror in Action* in a font that wanted to be humble. The queen did not take the dais; she watched from a high alcove, visible enough to be rumor, distant enough to be myth.

Enablement began with a slide of phrases: *Outcomes. Care. Resilience.* The words floated like lanterns. Then came charts—rounded, gentle, curated. They celebrated the "success of listening" and "alignment with worker voice." It was an impressive performance of consonance, the sound a hive makes when it wants to be seen agreeing with itself.

Blair, Pip, Sera, and Ilex stood near the back, slates tucked under an arm like tools brought into a gallery. Vetch took a place by the side rail, not as a guard this time, but as someone who had decided which room to stand in.

The senior officer spoke next. His voice was steadier than Blair had heard it. "We've paused Operation Fortify. We've authorized the Essential Checks pilot. Today we present Mirror's progress." He gestured to Enablement's charts.

They were fine, as far as they went—sentiment lines rising, complaint bars shrinking, word clouds shaped like approval. The room nodded in that low, agreeable way that nods at decor, not foundation.

"Outcomes," Ilex murmured, as if reminding the air of weight.

Blair stepped forward when the call for "field reflections" came. She did not climb the dais. She found a place at floor level where eyes had to tilt down to see her, where their necks would remember humility.

"We ran a comparison flight this morning," she said. Her voice carried not by volume but by the way the room had learned to listen when certain sounds returned. "Two corridors. Mirror Lane and Meadow Lane. We measured tend time, return time, output delta, spills. We logged care rendered without ritual delay."

The Enablement lead smiled the way one smiles at an eager student. "Wonderful. Please submit your notes to our repository after the session. We'll include them in the next sprint review."

"Or," Blair said, "we can include them now."

She held up a slate. Not high—just enough to pull certain gazes. Ilex stepped beside her with a second. Pip, tiny but incandescent, lifted a third. Sera did not lift one; she simply stood, steady hands folded, the argument made flesh.

The room's posture changed by degrees. Even a queen from a high alcove can feel posture. The senior officer paused, then nodded once. "Proceed."

Ilex spoke in the clipped cadence of physics. "Meadow Lane tend time: median 19 seconds. Return time: median three and a half minutes. Outputs up 18 percent versus corridor baseline. Spills: zero. Mirror Lane tend time: median two minutes, six seconds. Return time: median 12 minutes. Outputs down six percent versus baseline. Spills: two, both following protocol delays."

The Enablement lead cleared his throat. "We should contextualize—"

"The numbers are context," Ilex said, not unkindly.

A young overseer—the earnest one—raised his hand. "We also logged a care index," he said, surprising himself. "Care instances rendered within 30 seconds correlated with faster return and higher output. Instances delayed by protocol correlated with lower return and more error."

The lead's smile lost wattage. "Metrics must be properly authorized."

The senior officer, still steady, turned to him. "They are authorized by outcomes."

A murmur moved through the chairs. Not approval. Attention. The room leaned into weight.

Blair did not look up at the alcove. She pointed to Sera. "When a worker trembles, care now is governance," she said. "Mirror later is theater."

A representative from Mirror Lane—the one with the practiced smile—stood abruptly. "We provided comfort," she said, cheeks bright. "We listened. The worker felt heard."

"The worker waited," Pip replied, not sharp, not soft. "And a wing swelled when water could have cooled it."

Silence thickened. The kind that demands one more thing.

Sable's lamp glowed at the doorway like a quiet witness. He said nothing. He did not have to. The room had heard him before.

The Enablement lead recovered. "We appreciate field input," he said, returning to script. "To ensure quality, we'll spin up a Care Validation Board. It will define thresholds, gatekeep artifacts, and—"

"Gatekeep?" Sera asked, tilting her head. "From whom?"

"From misuse," the lead said smoothly.

"Care is misused when it is delayed," Sera replied. Her voice held no heat, only the gravity of someone who has stood somewhere longer than comfort. "And delayed when it is gated."

A worker from a far corridor stood up, voice shaking. "My lane added a reflection pause yesterday. Two minutes. I watched the corners of a cell dry while we waited for permission to help." She looked down at her feet. "It felt like we were measuring our shame."

The queen moved then—not much, but enough that light shifted on the dais. "The hive will not devolve into anarchy," she said from the alcove. Her voice was measured, an instrument that had forgotten how to improvise. "We proceed by process."

Blair did not look away. "We proceed by outcomes," she said softly. "Walls that do not sag. Bees that do not fall. Honey that does not waste. Care rendered in time, not permission."

"For whom do you speak?" the queen asked, not as challenge, but as a census.

"For anyone who carries weight," Blair said. "Which is all of us."

The queen was quiet. She did not descend. She did not dismiss. She left the sentence in the air long enough to show she had heard.

Enablement's lead attempted to resume narrative. "We propose a phased rollout of the Mirror framework combined with a Care Validation—"

"Window," the senior officer said, surprising himself again. "Not mirror. The word is window."

Laughter did not follow. Agreement did. The clerk in the second row crossed out "Mirror" on his handout and wrote "Window," as if renaming were a small hinge that might swing a larger door.

The meeting did not end with a vote. The hive rarely voted out loud. Instead, the room exhaled through a new phrase, and phrases in hives are the way decisions begin to take root.

After, in the corridor, an overseer with lacquered voice approached Blair. Up close, his eyes were tired. "You are efficient at making me look foolish," he said without malice.

"I'm efficient at making outcomes visible," Blair said. "Foolishness is a side effect of pretending."

He considered this like a man feeling a tooth and deciding whether it was loose. "If care becomes a metric, who protects it from becoming a slogan?"

"Everyone who must use it to stand," Blair said. "Slogans are weightless. Care is heavy. If it becomes empty, the body will tell you."

He nodded once, the smallest treaty.

Pip caught up, flushed. "We didn't break anything," she said, amazed.

"We moved something," Ilex corrected. "Breaking is loud. Moving is lasting."

Sera looked back into the chamber, where workers lingered without agenda. "They were listening," she said. "Not reflecting. Listening."

"Windows," Vetch said, joining them. "The word will stick. Mirrors still hang, but windows open."

"Then open them," Blair said. "And brace what the wind reveals."

She went to the meadow at dusk, unsure if the mentor would come. It did, arriving out of the lowering light like a question that had kept its appointment.

"They heard," Blair said.

"They saw," the figure corrected gently.

"And the queen?"

"She watched," the figure said. "Watching is how power learns without confessing it is learning."

Blair exhaled. "I do not need confession."

"You need muscle memory," the figure said. "Practice that proceeds without you."

Blair touched the ladder token at her band. "We are climbing out of holes we dug with our habits."

"Good," the figure said. "Be careful not to dig a new one with your certainty."

She almost smiled. "Then I will keep the questions large."

"And yourself small," the figure added, not as erasure but as instruction.

The colors on its wings dimmed with the day. "What is the next question?" it asked.

Blair didn't hesitate. "How do we make care durable?"

The figure rose, just enough to make air move. "Teach it to survive leadership changes," it said. "Embed it where metrics cannot rot it. Tie it to outcomes the council already worships. And then leave it behind you."

"Leave it?" Blair asked.

"Good carpenters leave houses that do not remember their names," the figure said.

It turned and disappeared into the slit of sky where the meadow kept its promises.

When Blair returned, Sable was waiting with a single sheet. At the top he had written: *Window Protocol, v0.* The bullet points beneath were plain:

- Essentials first. Wing, latch, weather.
- Care in time. Tend within 30 seconds; log tend time and return time.
- Outcomes only. Monitor walls, spills, outputs, strain.
- No mirrors without windows. Listening sessions require published outcome deltas.
- Open questions archived. No closing the circle without proof.

He looked at Blair over the paper's edge. "Draft?"

"Door," she said.

"Window," he corrected with a grin. "Doors are for later."

They stood in the corridor where the air was starting to learn a new route. The hive hummed the way a room hums after furniture has been moved—not louder, just truer.

Tomorrow would bring edits, politics, attempts to rename weight back into words. But tonight, the brace held, the ledger read nectar, and the questions, larger than any one voice, began to walk ahead.

They called it a draft, but the hive treated *Window Protocol, v0* like a weather change. Sable pinned a copy in the archive, Ilex etched it beside the vent map, and Rook recopied it into a one-page handbill for workers who preferred paper to rumor. No one printed banners. The words did not want height; they wanted hands.

Enablement arrived with edits, but for once they weren't all smoothing. They proposed a public log for tend time and return time, visible near the threshold. "If it lives in a corner," their lead admitted, "it will decay." They also suggested a training hour—not a seminar, but a drill where bees practiced care-in-time the way they once practiced oaths.

"Drill care, not compliance," Sera said. "I can tolerate repetition if it repeats what returns us to the meadow."

The senior officer surprised them by adding a clause: *If listening sessions are scheduled, outcome deltas must be posted at the door.* "No mirrors without windows," he said, the phrase having learned to walk.

Pip ran the first training. She kept it spare: a simulated wobble, a rinse with dew, a calm walk to shade, a return. She timed it with a piece of twine knotted at regular intervals. The young ones grinned—the way new flyers grin when fear learns to share space with skill.

"Within 30 seconds," Pip called, knot to knot. "Feel the difference? That's what time does when you use it."

Blair watched the practice take root the way a carpenter watches a joint seat—listening for the note when wood and wood agree.

The test came mid-week, the kind that usually writes policy by accident. Heat rose without storm, a thick warmth that made air feel crowded. In the west corridor—still outside pilot lanes—a supervisor had quietly reinstated a "reflection pause" after a near miss. He called it a "stability breath," a name so harmless that no one objected until it bit.

Two workers clipped lanes at once, not colliding, but close enough to trade panic. One froze in place, eyes wide; the other spiraled down, landing hard. A clerk reached for a form. The supervisor raised a hand for the pause.

Pip, passing, didn't ask permission. She knelt by the fallen worker with a vial of dew, hand steady. "Wing," she said. "Breath." Sera guided the frozen one toward shade, speaking with that thin, even tone that turns air back into air.

"Pause!" the supervisor barked again, louder, trying to reclaim the ritual by voice if not sense.

Vetch stepped between him and the workers with the stillness of a tree that has decided where the path must go. "Window Protocol, v0," he said. "Care-in-time takes precedence."

"This is not a pilot lane," the supervisor snapped.

"It is a hive," Vetch said.

The supervisor flushed and opened his mouth to counter, but the fallen worker flexed, nodded, rose, and returned gingerly to her lane. The frozen one's breath slowed and found a rhythm. The corridor felt itself release a held note.

Ilex appeared with a slate like a verdict arrived before the trial. "Tend time: 19 seconds. Return: four minutes. Output: preserved. Spills: none," he recited. He glanced at the supervisor. "We can post the deltas at the door or at the wall where fear likes to stand."

The supervisor swallowed, eyes shifting to the small crowd that had gathered. "Fine," he said, and it sounded like a nail relieved to find its hole.

That night, an attempt at rollback arrived dressed as reason. A memo circulated: *To avoid inconsistent practices, all care must be coordinated through the Reflection Desk to ensure comprehensive documentation and risk alignment.* It was unsigned; unsigned memos are a hive's way of floating trial balloons without confessing who exhaled.

Sable pinned it beside the protocol with a small gap so the wall could breathe between them. "Put claim next to counterclaim," he said, "and watch which one ripens."

Blair didn't argue with the memo; she argued with time. She and Ilex convened a short, public review under the threshold log: they posted tend-and-return times from the week, drew a line through them, and invited anyone to place a pebble on the side that felt like a life they wanted. Pebbles gathered on the side labeled *care-in-time* until the line stopped looking like a debate and started looking like a ridge.

The senior officer arrived, read the memo, read the log, and grunted softly. "I'll find the author," he said, not as a threat but as a chore. "In the meantime, the memo is paused."

"Windows," Pip murmured. "They let air through in both directions."

In the meadow, the mentor waited as if the day had unfolded according to an old calendar only it could read.

"Durability," Blair said without preface. "We're trying to make care survive conversion into policy."

"What is your anchor?" the figure asked.

"Time," Blair said. "Not hours. Intervals. Thirty seconds to tend. Minutes to return. Those are thresholds power cannot pretty into a slogan without tripping over outcomes."

"And where is care housed?" the figure pressed.

"In bodies," Blair answered, surprised by the speed of her own certainty. "In hands before forms."

The figure's wings warmed. "Good. Then build the house around the body, not the other way."

She told it of the rollback memo, the training hour, the log at the threshold. "We're teaching the hive to feel the difference between window and mirror," she finished, half proud, half afraid.

"Be careful," the figure said. "Mirrors will continue to hang. Teach those who like mirrors to stand near windows."

Blair laughed once, the sound brief as a knuckle tapped on wood. "That might be a lifetime's work."

"Then begin again tomorrow," the figure said. "Durable things are built from boring days."

The queen summoned Blair without theater. The message carried no seal, just a time and a place: the small room behind the high alcove where light arrived plain, unbent by ceremony. The walls were polished but not ornate; a chair stood beside the window rather than facing it. Someone here had moved furniture.

"You've made enemies," the queen said when Blair entered. It was not accusation, only inventory.

"I've made outcomes," Blair replied. "Enemies came with them."

The queen studied her as one studies a tool that keeps appearing in tasks one didn't know needed it. "They tell me you intend to replace mirrors with windows."

"I intend to open what was always closed," Blair said. "Mirrors can stay. They are good for grooming. But they are not for navigation."

"A memorable line," the queen said. "Useful for speeches."

Blair did not smile. "Use it only if you mean it in rooms like this."

Silence, long enough to be honest.

"The hive loves stability," the queen said at last. "Stability is how we call fear by a name we can say with guests in the room. Your questions threaten it."

"My questions threaten only pretense," Blair answered. "Stability built on pretense is the kind that spills when nobody admits the wall is bending."

The queen looked out at the meadow the way some look at old friends whose names they have not said aloud in years. "What do you want?"

"Durability," Blair said. "Care that survives leadership changes. Outcomes that survive slogans. A practice so simple the hive forgets it ever had to learn it."

"And what must I give up for that?" the queen asked, as if trying on a coat rumored to be heavier than it looks.

"Credit," Blair said, and felt the room tip. "You can sponsor the window. But you cannot own the view."

A small line appeared at the corner of the queen's mouth, a place where expressions practice before revealing themselves. "The council will rename it," she said. "They always do."

"I don't mind names," Blair said. "I mind weightlessness."

The queen placed a hand on the windowsill, as if to test whether wood still carried "window" without collapsing into "mirror." "We will formalize the protocol," she said. "We will post outcomes at listening doors. We will time care. And we will..." She paused, and Blair could hear the older word pushing against the new. "We will retire reflection pauses except when the risk is the talk itself."

Blair bowed—not low, exactly, but steady. "Thank you."

"This is not benediction," the queen said. "It is bargaining with a future that refuses not to arrive."

"Then invite it in," Blair said.

The queen turned her head, not toward the door, but toward the brace that had become legend when nobody clapped for it. "We will schedule a stress test," she said. "A day when we know the air will be cruel. We will run Window Protocol and see whether it is a story or a structure."

"Good," Blair said, though her stomach tightened. "Structure answers weather."

The stress day did not wait for scheduling; it found its own Monday. Heat and crosswinds arrived together, climbing the hive walls like arguments that had learned to shout. The corridors shook, not with collapse, but with opportunity for it. Supervisors looked toward mirrors; workers turned toward windows.

The first incident happened at the threshold—a young flyer, eyes wide, feet fast. She stumbled, not catastrophic, but enough to test a protocol's soul. Pip and Sera were there before time could form a bad habit. Dew. Breath. Walk. Return. Ilex logged a tend time that read like a prayer answered before it had to be spoken twice.

Across the comb, a different lane hesitated—an old overseer reaching for the reflection pause he had loved because it made him feel gentle while making others wait. The young overseer—the earnest one—touched his arm and pointed to the door where outcome deltas hung like new commandments. "Window," he said. "Or we watch numbers shame us."

The old overseer dropped his hand. Care moved. The corridor learned.

By dusk, tend-and-return times formed a line that Sable underlined with a quiet flourish. Spills: none. Strain: down relative to the worst heat. Output: stubbornly up. The memo author, whoever they had been, did not send another unsigned thought into the hive.

Blair breathed, and let the breath be ordinary.

That night, Pip fell asleep on the threshold, head on her arms, twine still looped around her wrist. Sera draped a strip of cool wax over her shoulders. Ilex checked the vents one more time, not out of distrust, but love. Vetch stood where guards stand when nothing needs guarding, which is to say, near enough to be useful, far enough to let the room remember its own strength.

Blair carried Sable's handbill back to her cell and pinned it above the tiny scale—*Window Protocol, v1.* The "0" had been crossed out, not with flourish, but with the thin decisiveness of a decision that plans to be tested again tomorrow.

She lay down without asking for the mentor. Questions hummed in the hive now, traveling without escort: How fast did we tend? How soon did we return? What did we brace instead of praise? What did we subtract instead of celebrate?

In the space where dreams take inventory, she saw the queen at the small window, measuring silence by what it allowed through. She saw mirrors still hanging, but next to them, windows that opened. She saw ladders tucked into bands. She saw the brace holding.

Morning would bring the last scene this chapter needed—the council's first attempt at codifying durability with a name it could survive and the test of whether Blair would accept the compromise. For now, the hum deepened into a note the hive could carry without straining.

And the note, finally, sounded like a house that had learned which walls were load bearing.

By morning, the council had a name ready: *Window Standard.* The communiqué arrived spare—no banners, fewer adjectives. *Effective immediately: Essential checks remain. Care-in-time is mandatory. Tend time and return time posted at corridor doors. Listening sessions must publish outcome deltas. Reflection pauses retired except where risk is the talk itself. Quarterly review by Outcomes Board.* The words wore work clothes.

Enablement brought a draft handbook. It was thin. Blair approved of thin. Ilex scanned the sections and nodded at the parts that let physics speak. Sera flicked her fingers across the "care-in-time" examples and corrected two diagrams with the quiet authority of someone who's carried shaking hands. Pip traced the tend-time table with her twine and smiled when the numbers matched what her knots already knew.

"Standards," Sable said, weighing the handbook like fruit at market, "are only dangerous when they seal. Leave them breathing."

The senior officer arrived with a new habit: he stood where windows threw light instead of where mirrors threw praise. "We'll run a codification meeting," he said, "fast and public. If it can't hold air in a crowded room, it won't hold in a crisis."

"Good," Blair said. "Make it dull."

He blinked. "Dull?"

"Dull is durable," she said. "If a practice requires a parade, it won't outlive the band."

The meeting did try to put on a hat. Someone from Communications had designed a tasteful crest for *Window Standard*—two rectangles and a ladder. "We can print pins," she offered brightly.

"No pins," Sera said, almost kindly. "Care should not jingle."

The queen entered without fanfare and took a seat on a plain chair, not the dais. The room shifted around that decision. Chairs do not change outcomes, but they do change posture.

"Proceed," she said.

Ilex went first: the structure—essentials, care-in-time, outcomes at the door, the board's role limited to tending numbers, not massaging them. He kept it short. Sera demonstrated the three-step care—the dew, the breath, the walk—and the two-step refusal—the gentle hand that stops a form before it replaces help. Pip presented the tend-and-return log, twine knots laid on the table like proof that doesn't mind being simple. Vetch explained the guard's part: clear a lane, not a conscience.

Blair spoke last, not to inspire but to anchor. "Windows are for seeing, not posing," she said. "If anyone tries to turn this into theater, measure it and you'll see it sag."

Enablement's lead, chastened by recent days, asked for two edits: a line on exceptions for complex medical events, and a note about protecting workers who render care from retaliation when they beat paperwork to a scene.

"Good," Blair said. "Both make the house kinder."

The queen glanced down at the crest the Communications bee still clutched. "Retire the pins," she said without looking up. "Print the standards. Put copies where hands can reach them."

The room exhaled the way rooms do when what needed saying is said by the person who could have said something worse.

Not everyone cheered. "We should keep a grace period," a lacquered overseer argued afterward, cornering Blair near the threshold. "Change is hard."

"Keeping someone waiting with a swollen wing is harder," Blair said. "Grace should flow to the hurt first."

He opened his mouth to offer a maxim; none came. "You make me repeat myself less," he muttered, confused by gratitude. "It's disorienting."

"You'll get used to it," Blair said, and meant it.

The first attempted co-optation arrived in miniature, as they often do. A corridor leader proposed *Window Ceremonies*—weekly events where teams publicly timed mock care and awarded ribbons for fastest dew. The idea was sincere and wrong.

"Ribbons turn care into performance," Sera said gently in the review. "We don't need faster dew. We need dew when it's needed."

"Replace ceremonies with drills," Ilex added. "Quiet ones. No applause."

The leader looked disappointed, then—after a half-sigh—relieved. "We can do quiet," he said. "It's cheaper."

The room laughed, and because it laughed softly, the laughter did not ruin the point.

Another attempt tried to turn *Window Standard* into an empire. A memo proposed a *Center for Window Excellence*, complete with a hierarchy and a quarterly summit. The queen herself red-penned the memo: *Too heavy. Keep practice light. Outcomes Board sufficient. Archive questions, not titles.* Sable circled the note three times when he filed it, the archivist's way of blessing a deletion.

Blair watched these waves and felt a new fatigue—different from the old heaviness of forms, closer to the tiredness carpenters feel after raising a frame: good work, solvable ache.

Pip found her at the threshold and tilted her head. "You look… not sad," she said, searching for the word. "Spent?"

"Bored," Blair said, almost delighted. "We are boring them into better habits."

Pip laughed. "Good. I can teach boring."

That evening, the queen asked for a short walk. No entourage. No script. They moved along a corridor where the tend-and-return log hung at eye level. The day's line was neat: a handful of marks huddled under 30 seconds, returns clustered under five minutes, spills at zero.

"My advisors tell me to claim this," the queen said quietly.

"They are not wrong," Blair replied. "Owning success is how systems bribe themselves to continue."

"And you?"

"I prefer you sponsor it," Blair said. "Sponsorship feeds practice. Ownership feeds pride."

They stopped at the east wall. The brace was due for another quarter turn; Ilex had marked it on the schedule. A small open circle, long since adopted by anonymous hands, glowed faintly in lamplight.

"You think I love mirrors," the queen said.

"I think mirrors love you," Blair answered. "They flatter most when you need them least."

The queen's mouth tugged. "You talk to me as if I were two people."

"You are," Blair said. "So am I. So is the hive."

They stood with that honesty until the room made room for it.

"What will you do next?" the queen asked.

"Inspect the rooms we were afraid to enter," Blair said. "The ones where mirrors still breed. Risk, audit, punishment. Teach windows there."

The queen's eyes flickered. "Punishment is not a room. It is a hallway even I avoid."

"Then we'll bring a lamp," Blair said.

The queen turned to go. At the door, she paused. "There are messengers," she said. "They whisper that hives beyond our fields have begun to sag under banners heavier than ours. If your windows travel, be careful where they open. Wind can be useful, or it can be a storm."

Blair inclined her head. "We'll teach hinges, not holes."

The queen left without flourish, and Blair let the space she vacated be just space.

Night came like a worker who knows how to leave on time. Sable filed *Window Standard, v1* beside *Window Protocol, v1*, adding two blank leaves labeled *v2 (for weather)* and *v2 (for politics)*. "Leave room," he said to no one, and to the future.

Ilex made the quarter turn on the brace and wrote the torque in the margin because he could not help himself. Pip coiled her twine, replaced two knots with a single knot she could feel without looking, and tucked it into a pocket where practice lives. Sera walked the long way home and stopped twice when she noticed workers hovering at doors, nervous about posting their outcome deltas; together they posted them, and the corridors sighed.

Vetch sat at the threshold and watched the meadow darken to the kind of black that belongs to good sleep. He had learned how to stand when nothing was wrong, and he found he liked it.

Blair returned to her cell and set two tokens side by side: the open circle and the ladder. Between them she placed the tiny scale that had once been only hers and now felt like part of the hive's pocket.

She did not call the mentor. She did not need to. Questions had learned to speak in more voices than hers: *What did we brace instead of praise? What did we subtract instead of show? What did we tend in time? What will we risk opening a window in a room that prefers mirrors?*

She lay back and let the hive's hum find her bones. It was not triumphant. It did not need to be. It was the sound of a house that had decided to carry its own weight.

Outside, a wind shifted—not a storm, not yet, but the kind of traveling air that carries news: distant hives fraying, familiar slogans failing. The meadow, generous as ever, waited.

In the morning, the chapter would turn: from windows in corridors to windows in rooms with locks; from care at thresholds to care where punishment had lived unchecked; from defending practice to exporting, it with caution.

But for now, a brace held, a ledger read nectar, and a standard lay thin enough to survive its own success.

5
Rooms with Locks

The hive hummed with a steadiness that was neither fragile nor triumphant—something in between, the kind of tone a house finds after furniture has been moved and everyone is still adjusting to the new weight. *Window Standard v1* was official now, copied onto thin slates, pinned at thresholds, even whispered in training corners where new flyers repeated "latch, wings, weather" with the cadence of something that might outlast ceremony.

But stability was not uniform. In the meadow corridors, essential checks and care-in-time had become habit. Workers tended one another swiftly, outcomes posted daily, tend-and-return times tracked with pride instead of shame. The logs glowed like honest mirrors—no slogans, only lines.

In older corridors, however, rituals still lingered. Reflection pauses survived under new names: *stability breaths, reassurance breaks, alignment moments.* Overseers clung to them with the stubbornness of bees who feared irrelevance more than collapse. One lane proudly announced it had *adapted* Window Standard by adding "pre-care forms," claiming the innovation increased "traceability." No one could say what it actually increased.

Blair felt the tension as vibration in her wings. The hive had opened windows, yes—but some walls still carried locks, and behind them shadows moved.

Rumors reached them first in fragments. A young flyer named Kel had spoken too freely during a listening session, questioning why *care logs* in his corridor showed more signatures than outcomes. Witnesses said the overseer smiled, thanked him for "candor," and escorted him away for "reassignment."

He did not return.

Officially, Kel was "resting in Recovery." Unofficially, whispers said he had been taken to *Discipline Hall,* a place few had seen but

DOI: 10.1201/9781003740056-5

everyone imagined: a chamber where punishment dressed itself as training, where fear was cultivated behind closed wax.

Pip heard the rumor in a queue and carried it like a sting. She found Blair at the threshold, eyes wide, voice brittle.

"They locked him away for asking a question," she said. "A question we would all have asked."

Blair steadied her. "Rumors bend with mouths. We don't know—"

"We do," Pip cut in. "Everyone knows. They just lower their voices when they say it."

Sera joined them, slower, her hands folded. "If Discipline Hall still stands, then Window Standard is theater."

Blair wanted to argue, but she couldn't. She remembered the mentor's warning: mirrors bend truth when framed too tightly. What, then, of doors that did not open at all?

That night, the circle gathered in the archive. Ilex spread fresh heat maps, but even he looked distracted. "The braces are holding," he said, "but that's not the only weight. If fear concentrates in one room, it strains the hive everywhere."

"Kel is gone," Pip said bluntly. "We can measure nectar and strain all day, but what do numbers matter if they can vanish a worker for asking?"

Rook shifted uneasily. "If we push too hard, they'll call it rebellion. Rebellion doesn't survive long in hives."

Sera's eyes narrowed. "And if we let fear have its own chamber, what survives then?"

Silence pressed down. Sable finally spoke, voice quiet but sharp. "Questions live in light. Punishment lives in dark. If you want to see what holds your hive, you must open the locked rooms."

Blair breathed deeply. "What good is a window," she murmured, "if some rooms still have locks?"

No one answered. They didn't need to. The words were enough to set their course.

The next day brought proof the rumors were true. A worker from Kel's corridor approached Blair in private, glancing over his shoulder. He pressed a scrap of wax-paper into her hand. On it, scratched hastily: *Kel. Reflection drills. Punishment. No outcomes.*

Pip read it and closed her eyes. "He's in there."

Blair folded the scrap, pressing it flat with her palm. Fear was a thick taste in her mouth but resolve stood behind it.

"They cannot call it Recovery if it produces no return," she said.

"They will call it whatever keeps the locks closed," Sera said grimly.

That evening Blair walked alone to the meadow, hoping for the mentor. For a long while, nothing. Then, out of the dark, wings shimmered faintly, not bright but muted, as if dust had settled on them.

"They are hiding punishment," Blair said at once. "Rooms with locks. Workers vanish. Questions vanish with them."

The figure regarded her, voice quieter than usual. "Do you want justice or change?"

Blair faltered. "Both."

"Justice punishes the past," the figure said. "Change prevents its return. But hives often confuse them. When they punish the past, they think they have changed. When they change, they forget to punish, and wounds fester."

Blair's chest tightened. "We cannot leave Kel to rot in silence."

"No," the mentor said. "But when you open locked rooms, be ready to see things you cannot forget."

Blair shivered. "Then we will not forget. That is how we survive."

The figure's wings dimmed further. "Be careful. Light reveals, but it also blinds."

And then it was gone, leaving Blair with only the meadow's honest wind and the weight of its warning.

She returned to the hive with her decision. "We go to Discipline Hall," she told the circle. "Not in secret. We request entry as part of Window Standard review. We ask to see their outcomes."

Ilex raised an eyebrow. "And if they have none?"

"Then we show the hive what nothing looks like," Blair said.

Sera's hands shook—not from fear, but anticipation. "Then the doors will open, or the hive will know they are shut."

Pip nodded fiercely. "Windows in every room. Or no windows at all."

Blair looked around the circle and felt the hum of inevitability. The hive had come this far. To stop at locked doors would be to admit that fear still governed. And she had learned, at too high a price, that governance of fear is no governance at all.

They did not sneak. Sneaking teaches the wrong lesson. Blair drafted a request on a plain slate with the weight of *Window Standard v1* behind it:

- Purpose: Outcome review under Window Standard.
- Scope: Tend-and-return times, recovery rates, spill incidents, strain deltas.
- Method: Unannounced sampling, direct observation, worker testimony with consent.
- Note: Reflection pauses to be suspended during review if they delay care.

Ilex signed as engineer. Sera signed as care lead. Vetch, after a long breath that looked like a vow, signed as guard for safe passage. Sable stamped the corner with the archivist's small open circle and the word *filed*—not to bless power, but to lock power to paper.

They presented it in the corridor outside the council chamber. There was no audience, only a clerk who knew which doors opened when. He read, frowned, then did something bolder than his badge required: he carried it in himself.

Permission came back, not enthusiastic, but official. *Review authorized. Two hours. Avoid disruption.* The word *avoid* felt like a curtain trying to play wall.

"Windows," Blair said to the circle. "Not wrecking balls." She looked at Pip. "Stay near me. Say only what you can carry."

Pip nodded, jaw tight. Sera tied a strip of cool wax around her wrist, a private reminder of what her hands had learned to do. Ilex packed slates and a vial of dew that had somehow become a symbol. Vetch adjusted his strap and felt the hallway remember that guards could escort truth as well as fear.

They walked.

Discipline Hall sat at the end of a corridor that had learned to make quiet sound like obedience. The door wore a modest placard: Recovery & Recalibration. Letters straight, wax polished, lies dressed like order. A receptionist with soft voice and tired eyes looked up.

"We're here for an outcome review," Blair said, holding out the slate.

The receptionist read. "You have two hours," she said, as if offering a drink in a drought. "No disruptions."

"Only windows," Blair said. The receptionist did not smile, but something in her shoulders loosened, the body's way of signing things it cannot write.

They passed into air that remembered too much talking and not enough help. Rooms beyond glass panels showed pairs of bees seated facing each other, one leading with questions from a script, the other answering in flattened tones. A metronome ticked softly—no pendulum, only a tiny lamp blinking at steady intervals. In the corner, a wall of forms wore the same posture as a trophy case.

"Reflection drills," Pip whispered, as if naming a ghost.

An overseer approached—polished, polite, practiced. "Welcome to Recovery," he said. "We're proud of our program."

"Then you'll be proud to show outcomes," Ilex replied, voice even. "Tend-and-return times, recovery percentages, spill deltas from units that passed through here."

The overseer blinked, smile thinning. "We track compliance with the protocol."

"Outcomes," Blair said again, gently. "Walls that do not sag. Wings that return to flight. Nectar delivered after rest. Your ledger for the hive."

"Our ledger is internal," the overseer said.

"Then open it," Vetch said, and the word sounded like a door remembering hinges.

The overseer gestured to a side room. "This way."

The ledger was tidy and useless, rows of attestations and signatures, a census of obedience. Ilex flipped pages, then closed the book with a small, deliberate finality.

"This does not know whether a worker ever flew again," he said.

"We support psychological readiness," the overseer said, slipping into a tone that had spent too long near brochures. "Confession reduces resistance. Resistance impedes reintegration."

"Confession to whom?" Sera asked. "For what harm? To what end?"

"For noncompliance," he said. "Failure to reflect, failure to recite, failure to align."

Sera's mouth compressed. "You are measuring volume where you should measure flight."

From the hall, a sound: a voice hitting the snag between answer and sob. Pip turned. The overseer moved to block, then hesitated at

Vetch's stance. They stepped into a room where two chairs faced, a script on a stand between.

The worker in the chair was Kel.

His wings were not clipped, but they were tired in a way scissors cannot cause—edges ragged from disuse, not damage. His eyes fell and rose in shallow arcs, a flight pattern learned indoors.

"Kel," Blair said softly.

He looked up as one looks up from underwater. Recognition took a moment to find a face to sit on. Pip had to clutch the door frame to keep from running to him.

"Window review," Blair said, keeping her voice as ordinary as possible. "We're here to count outcomes. Not words."

The facilitator—kind in the way paper is kind—stood reluctantly. "We are in the middle of a recalibration."

"We are in the middle of a hive," Sera replied. She knelt so her eyes met Kel's. "Do you hurt? Here?" She tapped her own chest twice, then her wings.

"Not hurt," Kel said, voice hoarse from overuse in the wrong direction. "Thin."

Pip's breath hitched. Sera offered a hand. "Stand," she said. "Walk with me to shade."

"That is not the protocol," the facilitator said.

"It is the window," Vetch said, moving a step so the facilitator would have to walk through him to stop it.

They stepped into a quiet corner where air had not been scheduled to hold feeling. Sera gave Kel the smallest sip of dew, then another. Ilex hovered close, not to minister, but to witness. Blair watched the metronome lamp blink against the wall and felt something cold crack behind her ribs.

"How long have you been here?" she asked.

Kel blinked, counting with difficulty. "Days," he said. "Maybe more."

"What did they measure?" Pip asked, unable to keep the tremor from her voice.

"My answers," Kel said. "How fast I confess. How well I repeat. How still I sit while they hold the mirror."

"And your flight?" Blair asked.

"They said later," Kel whispered.

Sera's jaw set, not anger—architecture. "We're going to tend now," she said. "Time me."

Ilex lifted his slate. Pip watched the twine in her head. Sera coached breath, worked stiffness from wing bases with a tenderness that had learned useless ceremonies by name and chosen to forget them. Kel's eyes cleared by increments. His shoulders lowered a finger's width, then another.

"Tend: twenty-four seconds," Ilex murmured.

They waited. Kel's breath steadied; his pupils widened back to sky. He flexed once and winced, not from pain—memory of control. Sera nodded. "Walk," she said. "To the door. We'll try light, then load, then decide."

The overseer hovered. "This is irregular."

"This is recovery," Sera said.

They moved to an open bay where a narrow lane could be flown without spectacle. Vetch kept the path clear with the particular grace of people who know how to be useful without being visible. Pip stood at the far end with an empty cell, not as test, as promise.

Kel launched—hesitant at first, then with the startled relief of a limb remembered. He wobbled once, corrected, landed by the cell and laughed—one small, astonished sound. He did not lift the cell. No hurry. He walked back, sat, and did not apologize.

"Return: three minutes," Ilex said, and the numbers felt like a soft cloth laid over a bruise.

Blair turned to the overseer, not unkind, not yielding. "These are outcomes. Where are yours?"

"We reduce disciplinary backlog," the overseer said, but the words sounded like a building reading its own blueprint aloud to a fire.

"Backlog of what?" Sable asked from the doorway. He had arrived without fuss, lamp in hand. "Sin? You have archived remorse and neglected return."

The overseer's mouth clicked shut.

"Show us your spill deltas," Ilex said. "Show us strain reduction after your program. Show us recoveries that sustained a season."

The overseer looked toward a back office that held more clipboards than chairs. "We don't… track that."

"Track it now," Blair said. "Or stop calling this recovery."

Kel sat between them, not as evidence, but as reason. He flexed again, cleaner this time, and looked at Sera with something like shame. She shook her head. "No. Not for you. Let the room be ashamed."

The facilitator, voice small, asked, "What do you do when someone refuses to confess?"

"Ask," Blair said. "Not what they did to the protocol. What the protocol did to them. Then remove what hurts and keep what holds."

The receptionist, who had followed them silently, spoke for the first time. "I can post tend-and-return times at the door," she said. "If that's what windows do."

"That is what windows do," Vetch said.

They had been inside 50 minutes. The hall had not broken. No formal order had been defied. But the air had moved in ways documents cannot stop. Sera led Kel to a bench by a real window and did not fill the silence with anything but breath. Pip stood guard, eyes still hot. Ilex sketched a data table so simple it felt rude. Sable opened the ledger and, for the first time that day, wrote something that would last:

- Care in time: 24s
- Return: 3m
- Outcome: flight resumed (no load)
- Mirror replaced by window: yes

He closed the book with ceremony so small it was only habit.

The overseer cleared his throat. "Your two hours are not finished," he said, as if offering a second glass of water after a drought announces rain.

"We'll use them," Blair replied. "On the floor."

She gestured to the rooms where metronomes blinked. "Suspend reflection pauses during review. Tend first, log second. If anyone asks why, tell them we are measuring what we claim to recover."

"You cannot change our program in a day," the overseer said.

"No," Blair agreed. "But we can stop it from hiding."

She looked through the glass at the chairs facing each other, the script between them, the lamp, the door. "Windows," she said. "Now. And then we'll ask for your outcomes in front of the hive."

The receptionist's tired eyes softened into something like courage. She reached under the desk, found tape, and held up a small sign she'd written on scrap wax: *Tend-and-return times posted here.* Her hand shook. Then it didn't.

Kel exhaled. It sounded like a held season letting go.

The last hour in Discipline Hall felt like standing inside a clock you've just wound backward. The metronome lamps still blinked at their tidy intervals, but their rhythm no longer commanded the room; breath did. Workers in paired chairs glanced up when Sera walked by, as if hearing permission they had not known to request. The facilitator scripts remained on their stands, yet a few pages folded themselves shut under the weight of watching.

Blair kept the review simple and stubborn. "Tend first," she repeated. "Log second. Post at the door." When an overseer tried to route a shaken worker toward a reflection station, Vetch stepped into the gap and pointed to the new sign the receptionist had taped where everyone could see it. *Tend-and-return times posted here.* The sign wobbled as if startled by its own courage, then held.

They sampled cases—quietly, consistently—across the rooms. A worker trembling mid-sentence; Sera coached breath, pressed dew to the soft place where wing meets shoulder. *Tend: 32 seconds. Return: four minutes, ten.* A forager hyperventilating when asked to recite the oath she had been punished for forgetting; Pip kneeled, whispered the window protocol's smallest rhyme—*wings, latch, weather*—as if to remind the body that competence existed apart from ceremony. *Tend: 21 seconds. Return: three minutes, twenty-eight.* A drone who had been told to "reflect on resistance," jaw clenched so rigidly his words came out like teeth; Ilex fetched a warm cloth, Sera changed posture from examiner to neighbor, and the drone unclenched. *Tend: 44 seconds. Return: five minutes, low load; reevaluate tomorrow.*

Not every case gave them neat lines. One worker flared at Sera's touch, memory recoiling from kindness because kindness had been used as a leash. They slowed, moved two steps back, listened. Sera guided care without contact; the worker calmed enough to choose shade. *Tend: three minutes. Return: deferred—consent required.* Sable wrote those last two words with a firmness that turned them from excuse into standard.

The receptionist posted each result, hand shaking only the first three times. By the seventh, her lines were straight.

"You're making us look chaotic," the polished overseer complained under his breath.

"No," Blair said. "We're making your order visible." She kept her tone level, the way one reads a temperature. "Chaos is what fear does when no one measures outcomes."

He stared at the fresh columns, eyes clicking from *tend* to *return* as if learning how to read where he had previously only copied. "We do not have a board to evaluate these numbers."

"You have doors," Ilex replied. "Numbers at doors make boards behave."

Halfway through their windowed hour, a voice rose down the corridor—thin, controlled, then breaking. Kel, escorted by Pip, had paused near a room where a worker was being asked to recount "non-compliant thoughts." The facilitator's script hovered between them like a shield that insists it's a mirror. The worker's eyes fixed on the blinking lamp.

"Pause," Pip said gently, the word repurposed. "Not for reflection. For water."

The facilitator hesitated. The overseer opened his mouth. Vetch looked at the door once, at the new sign once, at Blair once. "Window," he said, a guard's verdict.

Water moved. Breath moved. The lamp blinked into irrelevance.

They left with tables that would stand in light: fifteen cases sampled, tend-and-return times posted, two deferred by consent, no ceremonies performed in lieu of aid, one load tested, zero spills. It wasn't a season's archive; it was a day's proof that rooms with locks can be taught to breathe.

At the threshold, the receptionist touched the edge of Sable's slate. "Will you come back?" she asked, not in petition, but as someone negotiating terms with her own courage.

"We'll ask for your numbers next time," Blair said, nodding at the door sign. "We will ask loudly enough that silence costs more than posting."

The receptionist nodded. "I can live with loud," she said. "It is the kind whisper that hurt."

Kel stood beside Pip, less thin at the edges, more visible to himself. He had not flown a loaded lane; he had flown. He did not apologize for that.

"Public session," Blair told the overseer as they left. "Your outcomes with ours. Tomorrow." She gave him a slip of wax with the time and place. The word *outcomes* had finally acquired the weight it had been denied.

They reconvened in the archive. The room felt smaller around the tables not because the tables had grown, but because meaning had.

Sable placed the day's slate beside Window Standard v1 and the brace-torque log. He stamped the margin with two circles joined by a slender bridge. "For crossing places, we should not close prematurely," he said. "Discipline Hall will want to rename itself Recovery. Let it, if the bridge holds."

Pip sat, then stood, then sat again. "I wanted to break things," she admitted. "Chairs. Lamps. The blinking." She mimed the tiny flash with a twitch that made the rest of them simultaneously wince and smile. "But it would have made them the victims."

"Breaking teaches the wrong physics," Ilex replied. "Better to move load."

"Did we move it?" Sera asked, fatigue layering her voice without owning it.

"We shifted the center of mass," Blair said. "Tomorrow, we test whether the hive leans with it."

Vetch, quiet as wood, spoke from the doorway. "You'll need a flank. If the council can't erase numbers, they will try to erase context." He rolled the phrase *erase context* in his mouth as if memorizing a danger.

"Then we'll bring Kel," Sera said. "Not as exhibit. As witness."

Kel flinched. Blair saw it and adjusted. "We'll ask Kel," she corrected.

Kel nodded, then shook his head, then found a middle. "I can say one sentence," he offered, dry throat discovering it still owned consent. "They measured my silence, not my flight." He looked at Sera. "Is that enough?"

"It is honest," Sera said. "Honest is heavy."

The public session drew more workers than seats. The queen did not attend; the senior officer did, along with two members of the Outcomes Board and one from Enablement whose smile had learned restraint. Doors were propped open; the tend-and-return log from Discipline Hall hung beside Meadow Lane's daily outcomes, aligned so eyes could compare without asking permission.

Blair kept the order brutally plain. Ilex presented the numbers. No flourish, no rounding. Sera summarized practices: care-in-time, consent, no ceremony where aid belongs. Vetch spoke once, only to define his job in the sessions: "I clear space for care. I write down when anyone attempts to block it." He didn't look at anyone when he said it, which made everyone feel seen.

The polished overseer from the Hall opened his ledger of attestations, then closed it. "We do not have outcomes prior to yesterday," he said, each word like a knot coming untied.

"Begin," the senior officer answered. The man looked at Blair when he said it. It was not capitulation; it was a transfer of weight.

Kel stood because he had said he would. He did not approach the dais; he did not climb any furniture. He remained where the floor could hold him and said, "They measured my silence. Not my flight." He looked down at his hands after the sentence landed, shocked that one line could be both too little and exactly enough.

A murmur went through the room, the sound a hive makes when reality connects like a joint seated correctly. A corridor leader asked, cautious, "What will replace reflection drills?" Sera answered without speaking for a long time: she held up the tend-and-return log and let ink perform the simplest task: testify.

"Window Standard is not a metaphor," Ilex said. "It is a schedule."

Enablement's representative raised a hand. "We propose a swift transition: rename Discipline to Recovery; post outcomes at the door; replace scripts with short care-in-time practice; archive only tend/return and consent." He glanced at Blair and, in a small act of institutional humility, added, "Lead by those who actually render care."

"Approved," the senior officer said, voice not loud but final. He turned to the two board members. "Outcomes Board meets at the door next week. No slides."

One board member half-smiled. "We know where doors are," she said.

The session might have ended there, but co-optation does not sleep. A clerk in the back waved a hand with the nervous courage of someone who needs rules to feel safe. "What is the penalty for failing to post outcomes?" he asked. "We need teeth."

Blair resisted the urge to answer quickly. Teeth were always waiting; they did not need invitations. "The penalty," she said at last, "is loss of trust. The remedy is publicness. If a corridor fails to post, any worker is authorized to post in their place, and a guard is authorized to protect the posting." She nodded toward Vetch, who nodded back like a hinge functioning. "If someone prevents posting, the board meets there that day. Appetite for secrecy will fall when it must chew numbers in public."

The room absorbed the design. It was not punitive; it was oxygenated.

"And if a worker refuses care?" the clerk asked, earnest trouble inside a good question.

"Then consent governs," Sera said. "It is called recovery because choice returns."

The clerk sat down, not triumphant, but less afraid.

After, in the corridor, the young overseer—the earnest one—caught up to Blair. "I have been wrong in three different directions," he confessed, baffled and hopeful. "I thought mirrors were enough. Then I thought windows were fragile. Now I think windows are stubborn so long as hands keep opening them."

"Hands and schedules," Ilex said, overhearing. "Don't forget schedules."

The senior officer passed, paused, and did something memory would mark even if minutes didn't: he pressed his clipboard flat against the wall, wrote *care times* across the top in letters almost rude, and handed it to the receptionist from the Hall. "Post with this," he said. The gesture traveled through the watching crowd like an unstated amnesty.

Kel touched Pip's sleeve. "Can I ask for flight training tomorrow?" he asked, voice careful around possibility.

"You just did," Pip said, grinning like a life recovered in increments. "Latch, wings, weather at first light."

Sable lifted his lamp. "Archive the question," he said, and Kel laughed, the sound brighter than his body could contain.

When Blair reached the meadow that evening, the mentor was waiting with wings clearer than the night before, as if dust had shaken itself free.

"You opened a locked room," it said.

"We posted time in it," Blair replied. "Time bent the door."

"And what did you see you cannot forget?"

"That punishment can learn to pronounce kindness," Blair said. "And that kindness can be taught to refuse being used."

The figure's eyes warmed. "Justice or change?"

"Change," Blair said, and then—because she had grown enough to refuse absolutes—added, "and justice where it prevents forgetting."

"Good," the figure said. "Next you will learn export. Windows travel. Storms travel too."

It rose and drifted toward the horizon as if taking a measurement only the sky could read.

Blair watched it go, thinking of rooms with locks in distant hives, of the queen's warning about storms, of ladders and braces and schedules that make courage boring enough to last. Tomorrow they would plan how to keep Recovery from becoming Rehab with Banners. Tonight, she let the hum find her bones again, heavier and truer.

The hive, for the moment, was learning to count what counts—even in rooms that had forgotten numbers.

Recovery did not become gentle by decree. The sign changed, the ledger shifted, the doors learned their hinges—but habits still hid in corners. On the third morning after the session, a facilitator slipped a metronome lamp back onto a table. "Old reflex," she apologized, half to herself. Sera removed it without reprimand, placing a vial of dew there instead. "Old remedies," she said, and left the sentence open so the room could finish it.

The Outcomes Board arrived at the door as promised—no slides, no dais. They stood where postings hung and read the lines like weather. *Tend: 27s, 31s, 19s. Return: 3m10, 4m07, 2m56. Spills: 0.* They asked small, pointed questions: "When consent deferred return, did you follow up?" "What changed when the room was less crowded?" Questions that behave like hammers tapping wood, listening for hollows.

Enablement resisted the urge to narrate. They brought pencils, not applause. The senior officer had adopted a new habit of pockets—hands inside them when he wished to hold back his own voice. Twice he started to speak, then gestured to Sera, who explained a practice instead of a policy.

Pip ran dawn drills at the threshold for any flyer who wanted to remember that competence can be muscle, not recitation. "Latch, wings, weather—window," she said, adding the last word like a fourth check, and they grinned as if it were a secret worth not keeping.

Ilex, who trusted schedules more than sentiment, pinned a small calendar outside Recovery: weekly audit of tend-and-return logs, monthly review against corridor outcomes, quarterly stress test with vents warmed to honest discomfort. He wrote in the margin, *If numbers drift, investigate rooms first, then rules.* Sable drew a small bridge beside it for continuity.

Yet the backlash arrived, as all backlashes do—confident, delayed, convinced it had found a smarter costume. A circular came out of the upper corridors, typed on clean wax and signed by four names that liked being said together. *To preserve uniformity across the hive, all care events must be routed through a central Coordination Desk. Posting is to occur after validation to ensure fidelity.* The phrase *after validation* put a hand gently over a mouth.

The circular was legal. It was also wrong.

Blair took it to the queen's small room by the window. The queen read without comment, then set the wax down where light could touch it.

"Uniformity is not durability," Blair said. "And 'after validation' is a mirror that learned new words."

The queen's eyes moved to the meadow. "The signers are strong. They will say you endangered governance by inventing a path outside its teeth."

"I opened a window," Blair said. "Teeth are for wolves; we have bees."

The queen almost smiled. "We have wolves who wear bees." She tapped the circular with one finger. "If I crush this now, they will claim martyrdom and return with better parchment. If I endorse it, you will break windows to keep air moving."

"I will not break," Blair said. "I will open."

"What do you propose?" the queen asked, and the question sat between them like a hinge waiting to prove itself.

Blair pointed to the posting board outside Recovery in her mind. "A split: immediate posting of tend-and-return remains mandatory on site—time cannot be moved to the Coordination Desk. A desk may validate later for pattern and fraud but never posting. And the Board meets at doors, not desks."

"Write it," the queen said.

Blair wrote. The queen initialed, not lavishly. "I will not save you from every teeth," she said. "But I will keep windows from becoming ornaments."

The circular was amended by afternoon. Four names looked smaller on the new wax.

Hardliners found other angles. One morning, two guards—not Vetch—stopped Pip at a corridor border and asked for authorization to conduct drills. She held up her twine and smiled. "Practice is free." They frowned, unsure how to confiscate a piece of string, then stepped aside.

A facilitator tried to revive "reflect-and-affirm" by appending a single question to care: *What did you learn today?* Sera tested it twice and found it turned breath into performance. She replaced the prompt with, "What do you need now?" Recovery posted the substitution publicly; the old question looked theatrical beside a sentence that actually held weight.

A corridor leader proposed "Window Champions," a tiered role with ribbons and briefings. Vetch scratched his neck. "Windows don't need champions," he said. "They need hands." The title died without a fight, replaced by a schedule for who posts logs on which day.

Kel returned to flight in slivers. He refused a load twice and said the word *refuse* without apology. On the third morning, he asked for a small cell and carried it to the marker and back, landing with the gravity of a ceremony he'd chosen not to name. Pip didn't cheer. She touched the threshold once, a private salutation. Sera logged the return time and wrote *joy* in the margin before scratching it out and writing *steady* instead. Sable pretended not to see either word and filed both.

In the meadow that evening, the mentor came without glow—subtle as breath. "You are learning export," it said.

"We are learning to refuse export that turns into conquest," Blair said. "Windows travel. Storms travel too."

"And who decides where to open next?" the figure asked.

"Not a committee," Blair said. "A cadence. We will choose rooms by where fear is thickest, not by who invites us to pose."

The figure's eyes warmed. "Good. Another lesson: do not import storms. Other hives will ask for your standard. They will want to wear it like clothing. Standards that cross borders must be smaller than pride but larger than slogans."

"Smaller than pride, larger than slogans," Blair repeated. "We can send a one-page practice and a schedule. We cannot send a creed."

The mentor inclined its head. "Send ladders, not banners."

Blair laughed. "Sable will enjoy that line."

Two days later the queen tested edges. Without summons, she appeared at Recovery with the four signers of the circular in tow. No carpet. No fanfare. She asked to watch a morning.

They watched randomness behave. A veteran forager shook when a particular word in a script echoed an old fear. Sera closed the script and moved her chair three inches closer to the window. The forager steadied and finished a sip of water without spilling, which was more healing than most speeches.

They watched disobedience behave. A facilitator balked at posting a slow return time—afraid of how it would reflect on her. Pip posted it herself and wrote *consent deferred* beneath it. The facilitator stared, then nodded once: the public note had defended her better than an excuse would have.

They watched boredom behave. Three cases in a row were so ordinary that even the queen looked briefly tempted to add meaning where function held. She did not. She kept her hands in her lap.

At the door, the Board began their small tapping questions. One signer—bristling, polished—attempted to speak about the "larger governance picture." The senior officer, now a student of pockets, kept his own counsel and gestured to the numbers. Governance, deprived of mirrors, remembered how to look out of windows.

The queen's test arrived at noon. A worker declined care, citing embarrassment. Sera stood back and said, "Consent governs." The worker sat alone for five long minutes, then signaled with a finger: yes. Sera returned. *Tend: 17s. Return: 3m42.* The queen did not clap. She wrote something in her small book. Later, Sable would recognize the shape of the letters pressed through the paper when he filed the day's slate: *choice returns.*

That night, backlash tried one more time, the way small fires try dry corners. A whisper campaign claimed Window had become a cult—that workers now worshipped "care metrics" like idols. The rumor traveled on soft feet.

Blair answered with a short, sturdy broadcast posted at every door: Windows are not gods. They are holes in walls. If you need worship, try the meadow; it does not ask for it. She signed it with an open circle and left space beneath for anyone to add *questions kept open.* Workers did. They asked about rooms beyond Recovery—Risk, Audit, the quiet office where assignments were changed with a stamp and no explanation.

The queen sent a single reply, posted beside Blair's: Begin with Risk. Bring doors. It was not blessing. It was trajectory.

Vetch cleaned his strap. Ilex drew a map. Sera sharpened a pencil by tearing it with her teeth because she liked to feel the wood give way. Pip added a new knot to her twine at seven seconds—an ambition, not a rule. Sable laid out fresh slates and wrote at the top of one: *Rooms With Locks — v2: risk.*

Blair went to the meadow for breath and found the mentor already there, as if questions were now punctual.

"Justice or change?" it asked softly, a ritual that had learned not to become one.

"Change," Blair said, and then, stubborn, loving, "with justice where forgetting tries to hire ceremony."

The figure's colors did not brighten; they steadied. "Bring doors," it said. "And remember: a window is a promise to return with a door."

Blair looked back at the hive and tasted the edge of the next room. The chapter was not finished. The house had more weight to carry.

Tomorrow they would knock on Risk.

They began with Risk the way carpenters begin with a wall that may be load-bearing: slowly, audibly, in public.

A small sign appeared outside the office where assignments changed with stamps and sentences: Outcome Review — Window Standard v1. Beneath it, Vetch posted a guard schedule not to keep people out but to keep doors from drifting shut. Sera pinned a single page: *care-in-time applies to decisions as well as bodies.* Ilex added a ledger template—three columns, immodestly plain:

- Decision made (move, pause, reassign)
- Reason tied to outcome (wall, worker, weather)
- Return check (did the decision produce the result we said it would?)

"Three columns?" Pip teased.

"Three more than they have," Ilex said.

Inside, the Risk office smelled like warmed wax and old ink. Shelves lined with stamped slips; files stacked by season; a clock that ticked a little louder than it needed to. The chief risk officer—Reeve—wore a look Blair had seen on engineers asked to sit through sermons. He didn't dislike outcomes; he distrusted anyone who claimed them too easily.

"We don't do windows," Reeve said by way of welcome.

"You do," Blair replied, "but you've been calling them forecasts. We're asking to put glass in them."

He eyed the template. "Reason tied to outcome," he read. "We tie to probability, not to poetry."

"Probability is reputation dressed for a meeting," Ilex said. "Outcome is whether honey hit the floor."

Reeve's mouth twitched despite himself. "You want to audit our decisions?"

"We want to see if your stamps match your stories," Blair said.

"And if they don't?"

"Then the room learns," Sera answered. "Not the worker alone."

Reeve sighed like a man who knows a strong joint when he sees it and hates that it wasn't his cut. "Fine," he said. "Two weeks. Daily postings. No spectacle."

"No spectacle," Blair agreed. "Windows are not theater."

Hardliners arrived early to the new show that wasn't a show. One stood in the doorway with the circular-signer's posture. "Outcomes don't apply to risk," she announced. "Risk is what might happen."

"Then your postings will be short," Sable said from his corner, pen already open. "The rest of us will post what did." He drew a small bridge and waited for nothing in particular.

The first posting landed like a small stone in clear water:

- Decision: Reassign three flyers from West Clover to save energy.
- Reason tied to outcome: Forecasted crosswind + prior fatigue.
- Return check: Output fell 7% due to understaffing; strain up 12%; no risk realized.

Reeve stared at his own handwriting. "We made a safe choice," he said, as if reminding the air.

"You made a choice that looked safe," Blair said. "Now make a safe choice."

He scratched a note beneath his note: *reverse partial reassignment; post tomorrow.* The ink looked like someone learning to use it.

Next posting:

- Decision: Deny tool maintenance to East Brace until next cycle.
- Reason tied to outcome: Budget hold + low incident count.
- Return check: Heat drift + torque variance; incident probability increased. Action: authorize maintenance now.

"Govern risk like an engineer," Ilex murmured. "Not like a slogan."

A junior risk analyst hovered near the board, cheeks pink with a truth she hadn't been asked to speak aloud. "We always meant to do this," she said. "We only ever posted the stamp, not the return."

"Now the stamp learns humility," Sera said.

The hardliner in the doorway frowned. "Posting errors invites panic."

"Posting outcomes invites help," Pip replied. "Panic is a room with locks. We're replacing doors."

By midweek, something rare happened: the Risk board became less interesting. Decisions tied to outcomes; reversals logged with reasons; reversals worked. Reeve's face loosened into the kind of tired that belongs to good work. The clock in the office didn't get quieter; it merely mattered less.

So the backlash tried a sharper angle.

A directive slid down from a high room without a window: *To maintain consistency, all decisions about worker reassignment for "attitude risk" must be pre-cleared by Risk and executed immediately. Window postings optional.*

"The phrase 'attitude risk' is a mirror," Sable said after reading it once. "It throws your face back at you."

Reeve ran a hand over his scalp and looked at Blair. "If I refuse this, I make enemies you can't brace."

"If you accept it, you make rooms we can't open," Blair said.

They didn't argue long. Reeve walked to the posting board, wrote the directive at the top, and beneath it posted an empty return column.

- Decision: Pre-clear attitude risk.
- Reason tied to outcome: [blank]
- Return check: [blank]

He left the blanks visible like scaffolding without a building. Workers gathered, reading silence like a ledger. Vetch stood, hands behind his back, not blocking the door so much as preventing someone from stealing the blanks.

By late afternoon, the queen appeared—not with guards, not with Enablement. Alone. She stood by the board until the room noticed its own posture, then spoke softly.

"What is an attitude?" she asked Reeve.

"A rumor about a person," he said, and surprised himself.

"And what is a risk?"

"A rumor about a future," he said, surprising himself again.

"And what is an outcome?"

"A rumor that cannot remain a rumor," he said, and this time he smiled despite the shape of the day.

The queen took the directive down. "Post decisions that move bodies," she said. "Post reasons that accept weather. Post returns that undo your pride." She glanced at Blair. "Optional windows become mirrors. We don't need more mirrors."

The directive died without ceremony. The room exhaled. Hardliners did not cheer; they recalculated.

Kel arrived for his first official load after Recovery's postings had begun. He joined Pip at the threshold, touched the log like a talisman, and said, "Latch, wings, weather." Pip added, "Window," and they flew. Sera watched their return time as if it were a heartbeat. *Return: 3m18; load small; smile present.* She scratched the last two words out and left them visible anyway. Sable filed the day with two open circles: one for Kel, one for the work still unfinished on purpose.

In the meadow that evening, the mentor hovered already, a habit with a face.

"Justice or change?" it asked in the well-worn tone of a question that refused to age.

"Change," Blair said, and then, without apology, "Justice where forgetting would otherwise win."

"What did you learn today?" the figure asked.

"That risk learns windows by being embarrassed publicly," Blair said. "And that embarrassment is a poor teacher unless it ends in practice."

The figure's wings shimmered, a smile made of physics. "Where next?"

Blair looked back toward the hive, where doors had begun to appear in places that once insisted on walls. "Audit," she said. "The room that names truth after it's too late."

The mentor's colors dimmed kindly. "Then bring a clock," it said. "Teach them to measure while it matters."

The chapter might have ended there, but one more hinge needed testing. The hardliners, deprived of directives, tried a story. They told it softly across corridors: "Windows will invite storms. Softness will spill honey." Workers listened with the attention people give to weather forecasts written on rumor.

Blair posted a reply on a scrap of wax at three doors and one field marker:

Windows invite wind. Braces hold houses. Storms test both.

If honey spills, it will not be because we looked. It will be because we didn't.

She signed nothing. The hive knew the handwriting.

The queen added a line beneath, not as queen but as keeper of furniture: If storms arrive, we will not add mirrors. We will add doors.

That pairing traveled further than any decree. Vetch heard it in a murmur near the vents. Sera heard it in the way a worker accepted care without apology. Ilex heard it in the tick of the Risk clock, which now sounded less like a warning and more like a metronome for work worth repeating. Pip tied a new knot at five seconds on her twine—an aspiration she laughed at and kept anyway.

Sable filed a thin addendum: *Window Standard v2 (For Rooms With Locks): Risk postings public; attitude removed as a category; consent logged in care; returns audited at doors.* He left margins wide. They would need them.

Blair returned to her cell and laid the ladder token over the open circle, a cross that meant *climb, then leave space.* The tiny scale caught the lamplight and made a patient moon on the wall.

Tomorrow they would knock on Audit—the room that kept its own mirrors by writing history as if windows had always been there. The mentor's warning hummed under her breath: *teach them to measure while it matters.* She breathed once for Kel, once for rooms that had learned air, once for rooms that still thought darkness was neutral.

She slept without asking permission.

6
The Ledger and the Clock

Audit corridors were the cleanest in the hive. The walls gleamed with wax polished daily; the floors smelled faintly of ink. Ledgers lined every shelf, stacked in perfect rows like soldiers. Workers passed with hushed steps, as if noise itself could be logged as misconduct.

"Truth lives here," a clerk whispered once to Pip when she strayed too close. But Pip had peeked at the pages and saw only old storms written after roofs had already been mended.

Audit never lied, it was said. But everyone knew Audit always arrived late.

Blair stood with her circle at the threshold of the corridor, eyes tracing the shelves. The sight of so many ledgers should have steadied her; instead it made her stomach turn. Ink looked like weight, but it weighed nothing once the damage had already been carried.

"They recorded the east brace failure last season," Ilex murmured, pulling down a thick book. "Date: three days after we already reinforced it. Entry: 'Incident documented; controls adequate.'" He shut the ledger sharply. "Adequate after we fixed it."

Pip crossed her arms. "What good is a clock that only tells you the time after the sun has set?"

Sera touched the cover gently. "Audit gives legitimacy, though. Workers believe it even when they know it's late. It's comfort."

"Comfort is dangerous when it arrives after collapse," Ilex said.

Blair stayed quiet, listening to the hum of the corridor. It was an orderly hum, like bees rehearsing instead of flying. She thought of the meadow, alive with uncertainty but honest in its risk. Audit was the opposite: dead certainty after the fact.

The trigger came two days later. A spill in South Corridor—modest, containable. Workers rallied, braced, salvaged what they could. By the next dawn the cells were repaired, honey redirected. The hive carried on.

DOI: 10.1201/9781003740056-6

Two days after that, Audit posted a report. *Incident documented; controls adequate.*

Adequate, yes—but late.

Pip slammed the report against the wall in the archive. "They tell the truth like tourists—arriving only after the wreckage has been cleared. What good is that?"

"None," Ilex said flatly. "A delayed ledger is a lie written in tidy handwriting."

Sera frowned. "Not a lie. A shadow of truth. Thin, but real."

"Shadows cannot brace walls," Ilex said.

Blair leaned against the shelves, heart tight. "If the hive trusts shadows, they'll stop demanding light."

That night Blair returned to the meadow. The mentor appeared already waiting, wings muted, shimmering like parchment more than flame.

"Audit writes," Blair said, "but only when it's too late. They are praised for truth, but their truth is stale."

The figure tilted its head. "Is a ledger truth, or is truth a clock?"

Blair startled. "A clock," she said, almost instantly. "A ledger is history. A clock is now."

"And which does your hive believe?"

"They worship ledgers," Blair whispered. "Even when the honey is already swept."

The figure's eyes sharpened. "Then you must teach them: real-time outcomes are the only honest audit. Truth delayed is truth denied."

Blair's throat tightened. "They'll resist. They'll claim objectivity depends on distance."

"Objectivity delayed is complicity," the mentor said. "You do not watch storms from a distance. You measure the wind while it bends the trees."

Blair breathed hard, the words lodging in her chest like nails. "Then Audit must move to the door. To the moment. To the clock."

The figure nodded once, wings dimming. "Yes. But remember clocks must be wound. If no one keeps them honest, they will stop and still pretend to tick."

It vanished, leaving Blair staring at the sky's own clock—the stars, too far to help.

The next morning Blair carried the lesson to the circle. "We have to bring Audit to the door. No more ledgers after the fact. Live logs. Tend-and-return times posted as they happen."

"They'll never agree," Sera warned. "Auditors believe distance makes them pure."

"Purity is rot," Ilex said. "Outcomes rot when left too long."

Pip's eyes blazed. "Then we make a demonstration. We'll show what a clock can do beside a ledger."

"Comparison flight," Blair said softly, remembering the pattern. "One lane posts live. One waits for Audit. Witnesses will choose which truth they trust."

The pilot was set in West Clover corridor. Workers volunteered—tired of waiting for history to catch up. At the threshold, Ilex pinned a new board: *Live Outcomes—Post Immediately.* Beneath it: columns for tend, return, output, spills.

Across the corridor, an Audit clerk erected his own table, ledger open, stylus poised. "We'll record after confirmation," he explained primly.

"Confirmation of what?" Pip asked.

"Of incident, of accuracy. We cannot risk premature data."

Blair gestured to the board. "And we cannot risk delayed truth."

The first test came within the hour: a worker misjudged a turn, wing bent awkwardly. Sera rushed, dew at the joint. "Tend: 22s. Return: 3m11." Ilex wrote it instantly, chalk scraping against wax.

The clerk at the ledger looked uneasy. "I must wait for corroboration." He scribbled *pending review.*

Workers hovered, eyes shifting between boards. One showed ink drying in real time; the other waited.

By noon, the live board carried five incidents, all tended and returned. The ledger had two entries: *pending review.*

Pip tapped the log with her twine. "This is a clock," she said. "That is a history book waiting to be written."

The clerk flushed but said nothing.

By day's end, the difference was undeniable. Workers gathered by the live board, using numbers to adjust their shifts in the moment—rotating lanes, redistributing loads. Outcomes improved before the shift ended. The ledger caught up after dusk, tidy, belated, irrelevant.

Even the earnest overseer who once clung to Mirror paused to read the chalk. "I see now," he murmured. "Truth that waits is not truth."

The polished clerk from Audit stiffened. "Ledgers maintain integrity."

"Integrity without urgency is vanity," Blair replied.

The corridor buzzed with agreement. The hive was starting to see: a ledger that speaks only after is a liar that learned to write.

The next morning, Audit struck back.

A communiqué appeared on honey walls across the hive, stamped with the council's seal but clearly penned by auditors:

> The purpose of Audit is accuracy, not speed. Premature postings risk distortion, bias, and panic. Only verified ledgers ensure objectivity. All live boards are to be treated as supplemental, not authoritative.

Workers read the words with weary eyes. Some nodded; Audit had always claimed purity. Others muttered. Pip tore one notice down and shoved it into Blair's hand.

"They call windows distortion," she hissed. "They want mirrors again."

Sera rubbed her forehead. "Some bees will believe them. Audit has been truth for so long, even when late."

"Truth delayed is truth denied," Blair said, repeating the meadow's lesson.

That afternoon, a brace in West Corridor began to groan. It wasn't a collapse—just stress, the kind of sound that makes wings twitch. Workers shifted uneasily. Ilex moved to inspect, chalk ready.

"Stress increasing," he said. "Add vent relief. Reduce load. Log return." He posted the adjustments instantly on the live board. Within minutes, the pressure eased.

The Audit clerk scribbled furiously but refused to record. "We must confirm with senior review before documenting structural variance," he insisted.

"Confirm?" Pip barked. "The wall nearly sang itself apart!"

"Protocols prevent error," the clerk said.

"Protocols delayed collapse," Ilex countered, pointing at the board. "Numbers stopped it now."

Workers crowded the live log, murmuring: "We adjusted because we saw it. Without it, we'd still be flying heavy."

When the brace settled, the clerk finally recorded: *Incident pending confirmation. Controls adequate.* The ink looked obscene beside chalk that had already saved them.

By dusk, the hive was split. In meadow lanes, live boards thrived; workers trusted them. In older corridors, ledgers still reigned. The divide was visible in wings: some flew lighter, confident in posted outcomes; others sagged under faith in records that would arrive when their fatigue already had.

Blair convened the circle in the archive. Pip paced, furious. Sera looked torn, her hands restless on the table. Ilex stared at his slate, jaw tight. Vetch leaned in the corner, guard quiet.

"They'll call live boards rebellion," Sera warned. "Audit will frame us as reckless."

"They already have," Ilex said. "But the brace held because of numbers in time. Not reports in ink."

"Workers believe Audit is truth," Sera pressed. "If we tear that faith too quickly, fear will fill the gap."

Blair exhaled. "Then we don't tear. We show. A comparison flight—again. One corridor under Audit. One with live boards. Same day. Same witnesses."

Pip snapped her twine like a whip. "Then they'll have to choose which clock to trust."

Permission came harder this time. The council hesitated, caught between Audit's prestige and the hive's whispers. Finally, the queen herself intervened, her words clipped but unmistakable: *"Conduct your comparison. Outcome is the arbiter."*

Two corridors were marked: North Ledge for Audit, South Clover for live. Witnesses gathered: overseers, clerks, engineers, workers from both sides. The senior officer stood with arms folded, no clipboard, a pocket full of patience.

Audit arrived with a team of three, ledgers stacked, styluses sharp. They set up a long table with seals and stamps, the very smell of authority. Across the corridor, Pip propped the live board against the wall, chalk already dusting her fingers.

"Wings ready?" Blair called.

"Ready," Rook said, flexing.

"Latch," Sera confirmed.

"Weather clear," Ilex added.

They launched.

The first incident struck early: a flyer clipped a bloom, staggered, spilled a fraction of nectar. South Clover posted at once: *Tend: 18s. Return: 2m41. Spill: contained.*

Audit hesitated. The clerk whispered, "We need confirmation from two witnesses." They took testimonies, measured angles, debated responsibility. Fifteen minutes later, they wrote: *Incident confirmed. Worker fatigue. Controls adequate.*

By then, the flyer was already back in the lane, wings steady.

Witnesses murmured. Some pointed to chalk, some to ink. The divide widened.

Mid-cycle, a gust swept both corridors. In South Clover, three workers faltered. Care moved instantly: dew, breath, return. Pip logged: *Tend: 24s, 31s, 22s. Returns: 3m07, 3m54, 2m49. No spills.*

In North Ledge, two workers staggered. Audit hesitated, scribbled, argued. No one dared act until forms were half-complete. By then, one worker had collapsed, spilling his load across cells. The report read: *Incident confirmed. Root cause: environmental variance. Controls adequate.*

Workers who watched didn't need an education in root causes. They saw who had fallen.

By late afternoon, outcomes diverged like roads. South Clover's live postings showed small stumbles corrected, zero spills, outputs sustained. North Ledge's ledger recorded three confirmed incidents, two "pending," and one spill rationalized as "variance."

The senior officer stepped forward, speaking not with volume but gravity. "Ledger says adequate," he said. He pointed to chalk. "Board says improved."

An auditor bristled. "Ledgers are verified truth. Chalk is anecdote."

"Then anecdote kept the wall from sagging," Ilex snapped.

A young worker, no sash, no title, lifted her hand. "I fly North. My spill is in your ledger. My shame is inked. But in South, I would have returned. I know it. I felt it. I want the clock, not the book."

Silence fell heavier than any form.

That evening, Blair found the meadow darker than usual, clouds muting stars. The mentor appeared, colors dimmed to embers.

"They saw today," Blair said. "Live boards saved. Ledgers delayed. Workers want clocks."

"And what do you notice?" the figure asked.

"That Audit is afraid of being irrelevant."

The figure's wings flickered. "Fear will fight hardest when it is losing."

Blair clenched her fists. "How do we end their delay?"

"By making delay cost more than speed," the mentor said. "Tie outcomes to moments. Make every absence of posting visible. If a board is blank, let silence shame them louder than ink."

Blair nodded slowly. "Truth delayed is truth denied. Silence will be treated as failure."

The figure tilted its head. "Good. But remember: clocks must be wound. Postings must stay boring enough to last."

Blair's chest ached. "Then we'll teach boredom as discipline."

The figure's eyes warmed. "Then you have learned Audit's lesson. Not its history—its correction."

It vanished, leaving Blair with a hum that no ledger could record.

Audit did not retreat quietly.

Two days after the comparison, they announced a *Ceremony of Verification.* Flyers were summoned to the central chamber, where auditors would "demonstrate the rigor of ledgers" in front of workers, overseers, and even a few council scribes. The dais was set with seals, stamps, and parchment so heavy it bowed the table.

"They're staging objectivity," Pip muttered as she, Blair, and Sera entered. "A mirror painted to look like a window."

The first case was read aloud: *South Corridor incident, three days past, nectar spill observed.* Two auditors recited witness statements, cross-referenced logs, debated root causes. After 20 minutes they stamped the conclusion: *Incident confirmed. Controls adequate.*

The worker involved stood in the audience, bewildered. "But I've already flown ten loads since then," he whispered to Pip. "Why are they still talking about it?"

"Because they think talking makes time go backward," Pip said.

The next case dragged even longer. Charts unfurled, scribes copied phrases, and still no one asked whether the wall had bent again. Ilex slipped into the chamber, late, chalk dust on his hands. He leaned toward Blair. "West brace strain stabilized at dawn. Posted live. Corridor already rotated."

"And Audit?" Blair asked.

"They'll declare it 'adequate' sometime next week," Ilex said dryly.

By the fourth case, the crowd grew restless. A murmur rose, low and insistent. Workers shifted toward the doors where live boards hung glancing at the numbers posted that very morning.

"They're losing their audience," Sera whispered.

"Then we don't shout," Blair replied. "We let silence speak."

And silence did. When the fifth case was announced, half the crowd drifted to the door. By the end, the dais spoke to chairs.

Audit tried again with authority. A new decree appeared: *"Live boards must be reviewed by Audit within 48 hours to ensure alignment. Until then, all entries are provisional."*

Provisional. The word stung worse than a sting. Pip snapped it aloud: "Provisional care? Provisional tend time? Provisional breath?"

Sera shook her head. "If I wait 48 hours to rinse a wing, I may as well not rinse at all."

Blair posted a reply beside the decree, plain and short: Every unposted hour counts as failure. Silence is the report.

Workers nodded. They began chalking empty spaces when nothing was logged—*Gap: 1h. Gap: 2h.* The gaps spoke louder than stamps.

The crisis came sudden and sharp. A gust tore through West Corridor during peak load. Three braces moaned at once, one threatening to give. Workers rushed to reinforce, tend, and rotate. Ilex posted live: *Strain variance 17%. Load shifted. Return pending.* Pip logged two falters: *Tend 29s. Return 4m02.*

Audit arrived late with their ledgers. "We must verify before recording," an auditor insisted, stylus shaking as walls groaned.

"Verify with your eyes," Vetch barked, voice like iron.

They hesitated, trapped between training and truth. Then one—a young auditor with ink on his face—stepped forward. He grabbed chalk from Pip's hand and scrawled on the board: *Brace B variance 19%. Risk high. Reinforce now.*

The corridor leapt into motion, as if chalk had given permission their bodies already craved. Braces tightened, vents opened, loads redistributed. The groan eased into steadiness.

The young auditor turned, breath ragged. "There. Logged."

The senior auditor sputtered. "That is not procedure!"

"It is outcome," the young one said.

By dusk, the story had outrun the corridors. Workers repeated it in queues, in shade, in whispers near honey stores: *an auditor wrote in chalk*. The phrase carried more power than any decree.

Blair found the young man in the archive, staring at his ink-stained hands. "I broke rank," he muttered.

"You bent rank," Blair corrected. "Like a brace. Better to bend than to snap."

He laughed once, sharp and pained. "I thought objectivity was distance. Today I learned objectivity is speed."

"Objectivity is honesty," Blair said. "And honesty without time is vanity."

Sable pressed a slate into the auditor's hands. "Archive your sentence," he said. "You may not get credit, but you will get history."

The young auditor wrote carefully: *Truth posted late is not truth. It is obituary.*

Audit's authority fractured that week. Some clerks clung to ledgers; others posted in chalk with pride. Workers voted silently with their feet—gathering at live boards, ignoring stamped reports. Overseers who once defended Audit found themselves explaining why their corridors had gaps where outcomes should be.

The senior officer convened a review in public. He spoke less than usual, letting numbers fill the air. On one board: twenty incidents, all tended and returned in real time. On the ledger: five "confirmed," fifteen "pending."

"Pending does not brace walls," he said simply. "Pending does not return wings. Pending does not prevent spills. Pending is a mirror that shows yesterday's face."

He turned to the room. "From now on, Audit may keep ledgers. But clocks live at the door. Every corridor. Every day."

The queen addressed the hive that evening. Not from her alcove but standing in a corridor where a live board leaned casually against a brace.

"Audit has long been our memory," she said. "But memory alone does not prevent collapse. From this day, memory will be paired with moment. Ledgers will record. Boards will measure. Both are truth, but only one keeps honey from spilling."

She placed her hand on the chalk board, leaving a faint print. "Truth is not delayed. Truth is lived."

The hive hummed, low and steady, the sound of walls accepting new weight.

Later, in the meadow, the mentor appeared brighter than in weeks, wings gleaming as if pleased.

"They chose the clock," Blair said. "Audit still writes, but now windows open in time."

"And what do you notice?"

"That reform always bends toward co-optation unless tied to outcomes," Blair said. "Every room we open tries to dress in mirrors again."

The mentor's wings shimmered. "And your story?"

Blair looked toward the hive. "Truth is not a book. It is a clock. A book records storms. A clock tells you when they arrive."

The figure nodded. "And storms?"

"They're coming," Blair whispered. "The queen warned. Other hives already sag. Our windows may not hold if the wind is strong."

The mentor leaned closer. "Then brace. And remember: clocks not only tell time. They tell when time is running out."

It vanished into the dark, leaving Blair with a chill that was not entirely fear—more like anticipation.

Audit did not surrender with words it could sign. It tried one last trap with words it could whisper.

A memo without authorship drifted down corridors like lint: *"To preserve independence, auditors must refrain from interacting with incidents in progress. Any chalk markings by Audit staff shall be considered advisory only and must be superseded by verified ledgers."* The phrase *refrain from interacting* put handcuffs on the very hands the hive had just learned to trust.

Workers read it, then checked the door boards and kept working. Chalk had become the hum's handwriting.

Sera pinned a short reply where the memo tried to settle: Care does not wait for permission. Audits that cannot touch are stories about courage told from far away.

Reeve, the chief risk officer, stood in the doorway of his office and reread the whisper-memo twice. "Independence is not abstinence," he said to no one in particular. "It's posture with a clock."

He walked to the Audit corridor and posted his own line beneath Sera's: If objectivity requires delay, it is not objective. It is ornamental. Then, in smaller writing, he added—*Reeve (Risk).*

The signature mattered. The memo wilted faster than rumor could water it.

The next morning, the Outcomes Board did something almost impolite: they arrived at the Audit corridor unannounced and asked to see gaps.

"Show us every blank period in the last seven days," the senior officer said.

A clerk shuffled pages. The ledger recorded confirmations and stamps with crisp precision; it did not record waiting. Sable leaned over the table and tapped margins that were always wide and always empty. "If you do not archive absence," he said mildly, "absence learns impunity."

The young auditor—the one with ink on his face who had reached for chalk—brought a stack of slates he'd started in secret: gap logs, hand-scratched. He set them down where the room could see.

- North Ledge: gap 3h (no postings during brace strain); reason cited: awaiting confirmation.
- South Clover: gap 0h (live board continuous).
- West Corridor: gap 1h (Audit absent during gust event); reason cited: staffing.
- Hall (Recovery): gap 0h (care postings continuous).

The senior auditor stiffened. "Those are unofficial."

The senior officer looked up. "They are visible."

The room turned, ever so slightly, toward the slates. Visibility has gravity.

"Post them," Blair said. She didn't raise her voice. She didn't have to. "At the door."

The senior auditor hesitated. The young one didn't. He lifted the stack and walked to the threshold. Vetch stepped into place, not blocking, simply keeping the air clean. The slates went up. Gap by gap, the story of delay attached itself to wood, which is less forgiving than rumor.

"Post a plan beside each gap," Ilex added. "Clocks not only tell time; they tell you what to do before the hour passes."

By afternoon, the first plans appeared, blunt and decent:

- Staffing cross-coverage for gust days.
- Auditor-on-call schedule at doors, not desks.
- If gap exceeds 30 minutes, Outcomes Board meets there.

Audit had not lost its ledgers; it had gained a conscience.

Hardliners regrouped in the one place windows can't fix: meanings. They began to say, *"live data is noisy."* They began to treat chalk like gossip and stamps like proof.

Pip answered without a speech. She added a small fourth column to every door board: Revision—times when an initial post had been corrected, what changed, and why. The column was not a surrender to the ledger; it was an admission that honesty sometimes needs an eraser.

The first revision read:

- *Tend: 26s → 29s (timer misread; corrected by witness). Return unchanged.*

Below it, Sera wrote, Correction is care for truth.

A worker from a far corridor traced the word with a fingertip. "I trust this," she said. "Because it breathes."

That week, the queen requested a walk—not in a chamber, but along the eastern run where vent-cool air met the edge of afternoon heat. She carried no retinue, only a small book whose edges had learned her hand.

"You have made windows stubborn," she said without preface. "Enough that they stay open even when nobody is watching."

"That was the point," Blair said. "A good window does not require applause."

They stopped by a brace that had become almost myth. Ilex approached, torque wrench in pocket, as if summoned by the wall. He nodded to the queen, adjusted the quarter turn he'd planned, and logged it on the door board—time, torque, reason. No one asked for a stamp. The act looked like prayer to a god that accepted physics.

"You've heard it then," the queen said softly, gaze sliding toward the meadow.

"The rumors?" Blair asked.

"Not rumors," the queen corrected. "Messengers." She lifted the book. Inside, scribbled reports from scouts and traders: hives beyond the fields where banners multiplied while braces thinned; a colony that silenced its windows and called storms blasphemy; another that measured with clocks and still lost a wall because their numbers hung in rooms nobody walked past.

Pip arrived with twine still around her wrist, saw the book, and grew quiet.

"Windows invite wind," the queen said. "Are you prepared to welcome the wind we did not order?"

"We prefer wind to stale air," Blair said.

"Wind is not polite," the queen replied. "It will throw your papers and test your patience. It will make brave workers look foolish for a morning."

"Then we will be brave in the afternoon," Sera said, catching up, breath even. "And foolish in the evening if we must. But we will not be late."

The queen's mouth tilted at the corner. "The clocks at doors give me courage," she admitted, a sentence that would have sounded like heresy in earlier chapters. "But courage has neighbors: humility and preparation."

"Preparation has neighbors too," Ilex said. "Calendar and maintenance."

"Good," the queen said. "Then I will ask this of you: codify boredom. Make a dull schedule for windows—their posting, their corrections, their audits. When storms arrive, dull schedules do not panic."

Blair nodded. "We can write *Window Standard v3: clocks and dullness.*"

"Rename it," the queen said dryly. "Communications will struggle to sell dullness."

Sable, who had been listening like a wall with ears, offered from behind them, "*The Ledger and the Clock—Practice Guide.*"

The queen's brow lifted. "That, I can sign."

They returned to the corridor to find Audit attempting a final performance: a *Ledger Parade*—a line of auditors carrying books past door boards, stamping cases as they went, as if motion could substitute for moment. It might have worked a season ago. Now it looked like a costume from a play that had closed.

The young auditor stepped out of line and set his book on a stool by a board. He opened it to a blank page and wrote across the top: Live Ledger—Synchronized. Then he copied the day's chalk into the book in ink, including the revisions, with the time of each entry. He did not change a thing.

"Ledger need not be late," he said aloud, to his elders and to himself. "It can be parallel."

A murmur of relief moved through the line like a joint reseating. Elders grumbled, but their grumbling sounded old even in their own ears.

"Parallel truth," Blair said. "Book and board."

"Clock first," Pip added.

"Clock first," repeated the senior officer, who had appeared and chosen a place to stand that gave the sentence weight without spectacle.

The parade dissolved into work.

That night, the archive felt less like a sanctuary and more like a shop after closing: tools hung, slates stacked, a list on the wall for tomorrow. Sable placed a thin folder beside the thicker ones: *The Ledger & the Clock—v1 (door posting, live ledger, gaps, revisions).* In the margin he left a deliberate blank labeled *for storms.* He did not need a prophet to predict he would use it soon.

Blair stepped outside with the mentor's absence at her shoulder; lately its visits had become less necessary and more precise. The sky had a texture that meant weather.

"What else will they try?" Pip asked, leaning on the threshold.

"Names," Sera said. "They will rename clocks until they seem ornamental."

"Then we'll call them alarms," Ilex said, half-smiling, and wrote *alarm check* beside *tend* and *return* as a placeholder that might stick or might not.

Vetch took first watch without being asked. Guards had learned to guard practice.

A breeze came—the kind that carries other hives' dust. It tasted of old banners and new fear. The door boards fluttered lightly, then settled as if reminding the air that they were attached to walls.

Blair felt the hum change key, not to panic but to readiness. The queen's book, the rumor of storms, the way ledgers had learned to write beside chalk—it all arranged itself into a promise and a test.

"Truth is a clock," she said quietly, almost to herself. "And clocks, if trusted, will tell you when time is running out."

"That's what alarms are for," Pip answered, knotting twine at exactly five seconds and snipping the tail.

The hive slept the productive kind of sleep that makes morning inevitable. In the distance, something large rearranged itself. It did not yet announce its name.

The queen called the gathering without grandeur. No banners, no dais. Only a wide corridor where door boards leaned side by side—Recovery, Risk, Audit—each crowded with chalk. Ledgers rested beneath them, open and parallel, no longer adversaries but echoes.

"Window Standard has grown into practice," the queen began. "But practice must endure beyond zeal. Storms do not ask if you are inspired. They ask if you are prepared."

Blair felt the hive's silence lean forward.

"We codify today," the queen said. "Boards at doors, posts in real time, gaps logged, revisions recorded, ledgers kept parallel but not supreme. This is not optional. This is clock and ledger together."

Her gaze slid across the room, past auditors and overseers, to workers who had carried chalk like contraband. "Truth is a clock. From now on, clocks will be wound."

The codification was dull, by design.

Ilex drafted schedules: *Postings at shift start, mid-cycle, and end. Brace strain logged hourly, or on incident. Guards assigned for continuity.* Sera wrote procedures for consent, corrections, deferred returns. Pip added drills—quick, repetitive, boring enough to embed in muscle memory.

Enablement tried to embellish. "We could name it the Integrated Assurance Window Framework," their lead suggested brightly.

"Call it what it is," Blair said. "The Ledger and the Clock."

Reeve chuckled, surprising even himself. "I like dull. Dull means reliable."

The queen signed the page. "So be it. Ledger and Clock. Dull, stubborn, alive."

The hardliners made one last appeal. "If everything posts live, mistakes will multiply. Workers will panic."

Sera shook her head. "Workers panic when no one tells them anything. Mistakes corrected in light are smaller than mistakes hidden in shadow."

"Noise will bury signal," another protested.

Ilex tapped the revision column. "Noise already has a column. Signal learns from it."

Vetch leaned forward, voice quiet but hard. "And any who block posting will meet me first. That's governance too."

The appeal died where it stood.

The first test of codification arrived not from inside but outside.

A messenger returned from the north fields, wings ragged from distance. He landed hard at the archive, clutching a wax tablet. Sable took it, read, and called for Blair.

The tablet told a story in hurried lines: another hive, larger than theirs, had banned windows outright. Leaders called them "dangerous distractions." Rituals multiplied. Banners proclaimed resilience. Braces cracked. Honey spilled. Workers silenced. "Storm overcame us," the message ended. "We seek shelter."

Blair's stomach sank. The storm was not rumor anymore. It was arrival.

She carried the tablet to the queen. The queen read, face still. "So it begins," she said. "Our windows will be judged not only by our hive, but by others."

That night, the door boards trembled with messages scratched by new hands:

- *How do we help those who seek us?*
- *Can windows travel without breaking?*
- *What if storms arrive faster than clocks can count?*

Pip added her own: *What good is a window if the wind blows it off its hinges?*

Sable wrote beneath hers: *Then build hinges stronger than pride.*

Blair touched the chalk, thinking of the mentor's warnings. Clocks must be wound. Windows must be braced. Pride must never be allowed to call itself proof.

She looked at the boards and whispered, "This is the hum before the storm."

The mentor came at dawn. Its wings glowed faintly, as if carrying another hive's dust.

"They codified dullness," Blair said. "Ledger and clock together. Gaps posted, corrections logged. The hive believes."

"And what do you notice?" the figure asked.

"That truth endures only if it is boring enough to repeat," Blair said. "Excitement fades. Schedules stay."

The figure nodded. "Good. But storms care little for schedules. They will tear at hinges. They will test whether dullness can flex."

Blair exhaled. "The north hive has already fallen."

The figure's colors dimmed. "Then your windows will not be judged only by you. They will be judged by those who arrive desperate, and by those who resent your survival."

Blair swallowed. "How do we brace against envy and fear?"

"By making your clocks generous," the mentor said. "Teach them to ring not only for you, but for any who listen. If storms are shared, alarms must be shared too."

It vanished, leaving the meadow hushed as if holding its own breath.

At the evening gathering, Blair repeated the lesson. "Storms will not ask if we are ready. They will ask if we are open. The Ledger and the Clock is not just for us. It must be written so others can carry it."

Reeve nodded grimly. "Export without conquest. One page, not a banner."

Sera added, "Teach outcomes, not ceremonies. Care, not titles."

Pip tied another knot in her twine. "And teach alarms, not excuses."

The queen raised her book. "Storms travel. So must practice. Prepare to share."

As night settled, the hive's hum shifted into a lower key—anticipatory, braced. Workers checked door boards as they passed, posting without being told, correcting without shame, trusting the clock more than the ledger and the ledger only as a shadow of what had already been seen.

In her cell, Blair laid the open circle and the ladder token beside the tiny scale. She added a scrap of chalk, worn down from a day's postings.

Together they looked like a kit for survival: unfinished, ascending, balanced, timed.

She closed her eyes and heard the first faint signal of distant thunder. Not a rumor. Not a story. A storm.

And she whispered the sentence that had become the hive's truth:

> "Truth is not a book. It is a clock. And clocks tell you when time is running out."

7
Storm Signals

The message from the north arrived in fragments, carried by bees whose wings looked like torn cloth. They collapsed at the threshold, eyes wide, carrying little more than breath.

Sera bent first, dew already in hand. Pip steadied the weakest, murmuring the simple rhyme—*latch, wings, weather*—as if to remind bodies that they were more than freight. Ilex fetched slates. Blair crouched low, close enough to catch words before they dissolved.

"Storm," one whispered. "Walls… banners… silence. We asked for windows. They sealed them. Then—" His voice broke.

Another added, "Honey lost. Brace fell. Leaders blamed… wind. Not themselves."

The hive gathered in tense rings. Everyone had heard rumors of storms. But this was no rumor. This was weather with a name.

The queen convened them by evening. She stood not in the alcove but in a corridor where door boards leaned heavy with chalk. The sight alone felt like a choice.

"Our reforms will be judged not by ceremonies," she said, voice low but carrying, "but by storms. This hive will learn whether windows are weakness or strength. And we will learn quickly, for weather travels."

No one cheered. Cheering belongs to festivals. This was the hush of a brace that knows wind is coming.

The first scouts confirmed it by dawn. Dark clouds moved low across the meadow, not in sheets but in restless fragments. Winds tugged at flowers before bees reached them. The hum of the hive shifted, a note lower, like a throat bracing.

Door boards filled with chalk questions:

- *Will windows hold?*
- *Do we close them to keep the wind out?*
- *What good is a posting if the storm washes it away?*

DOI: 10.1201/9781003740056-7

Hardliners took the chalk too, scrawling in heavy lines: *Seal doors. Lock windows. Silence survives.*

Pip erased one, jaw tight. "Silence kills," she muttered, writing instead: *Alarms save lives.*

Blair read the boards, heart thudding. Reform had been tested in politics, in rituals, in locked rooms. Now nature itself had come to grade their work.

The circle met in the archive as rain tapped faintly at the walls. Ilex spread sketches of braces, red lines marking stress points.

"We reinforce here, here, and here," he said, tapping with a stylus. "Double shifts. Vent adjustments every two hours. Survive first, debate later."

Sera shook her head. "Survival without openness is only delay. If we close windows, the hive may last a season, but fear will own us again."

"Fear doesn't matter if walls fall," Ilex countered.

"Fear matters because it makes walls fall faster," Sera snapped.

Pip cut in, eyes bright with conviction. "Then we prove windows in the storm. Alarm checks, live postings, everything in view. Let the wind see we are not hiding."

Blair felt the weight of all three voices—engineer, healer, young fire. She clenched her fists. "If windows fail, reforms collapse. If we close them, fear wins. Both destroy us."

Silence held the archive. Sable finally placed his lamp on the table. "Then ask not if windows fail," he said. "Ask how we brace windows, so they do not."

That night Blair walked to the meadow, rain already streaking her wings. The mentor appeared, wings heavy with dust carried from storms elsewhere.

"Do you want to be safe, or to be true?" it asked, voice flat as thunder.

Blair swallowed. "Both. But if I must choose, truth. Because safety without truth is just delay."

The figure's eyes narrowed. "Storms reveal whether your braces were practice or posture. This will not be rehearsal. If windows are weak, they will shatter."

"Then we brace them," Blair said fiercely. "We brace with schedules, logs, consent, outcomes—everything dull enough to survive."

The mentor tilted its head. "Good. Remember: storms do not care about poetry. They care about hinges."

It vanished, leaving only the roar of wind against grass, a rehearsal already begun.

By morning, the stormfront struck.

The hive shook in its combs, walls moaning under strain. Rain seeped into cracks, dripping into cells. Winds pressed at braces until they groaned like old bones. Workers staggered mid-flight, some spun sideways by gusts.

Hardliners shouted through the corridors: "Seal doors! Close boards! Hide the windows!" They began nailing shutters, pressing wax into gaps.

Vetch tore the first seal down with hands like stone. "Windows are alarms!" he roared. "Without them we are blind!"

Pip darted to a board nearly hidden by wax, scraping it free, chalking in wide strokes: *Strain variance rising—vent relief now!* Workers scrambled, adjusted, and the wall sighed easier.

Sera sprinted to a faltering flyer, tending her within seconds. "Tend: 27s. Return: 3m40!" she shouted, chalk flying as fast as dew. The posting glowed in lamplight, a flare in rain.

Audit hesitated in the chaos, styluses hovering. Then the young auditor—the one who had once broken rank—grabbed chalk again and scrawled: *Brace C variance 24%! Reinforce now!*

The corridor moved at once, not waiting for stamps. Braces tightened. Strain eased.

Numbers had become commands.

Blair stood at the threshold, rain soaking her hair, watching chalk streak boards faster than water could wash them. Live postings spread like veins: tend times, brace strain, returns, spills prevented.

Hardliners tried again to shout them down, voices ragged: "Noise! Panic! Close!"

But the hive wasn't listening. Workers read the boards and moved with precision. They had no appetite for silence anymore.

Blair whispered to herself, to the storm, to the hive: "Truth is a clock. And the clock is ringing."

And the hive, battered, humming low, answered by surviving.

Wind chewed the edges of the hive like a patient animal. It didn't howl; it insisted. The corridors bowed and unbowed. Boards rattled against braces. The chalk lines bled, then dried, then were written again. Boredom had become choreography; now choreography became survival.

"North vent—two turns open," Ilex called, voice clipped, rain biting his cheeks. He wrote it on the nearest board because speaking wasn't enough anymore. "Brace B, quarter-turn tighten; log torque; post strain delta."

Workers moved without waiting for applause. Vetch cleared a path with the stubborn grace of a tree refusing to uproot. Pip flew low along the boards with a stub of chalk in her fist, refreshing what the water smudged, replacing what fear tried to rename.

Sera tended in zigzags—dew, breath, walk, return—her hands small arguments against the storm's thesis that time belongs to the loudest.

On a higher tier, a hardliner overseer hammered a shutter over a window slit and shouted, "Seal it or we'll lose the corridor!"

Pip stopped, chest heaving. "Windows are alarms!" she yelled. "You are nailing a bell to the wall."

He sneered. "Alarms cause panic."

"Panic is what you get when bells ring from inside your pocket," she shot back, and ripped the shutter off with a violence that surprised even her. The board behind it shone with urgent, useful truth: *Strain variance 21%—vent relief working. Maintain.*

The overseer opened his mouth, then looked at the line and closed it. Sometimes reality is the only insult that persuades.

A squall hit sideways. Two flyers skidded into each other midlane; a third pinwheeled toward the wall. Sera and Vetch crossed in a snap, a practiced knot. "Tend: 19s," Ilex posted before anyone asked. "Return: 2m58. Return: 3m13." No ceremony, no commentary, just the clock telling breath how to behave.

The young auditor appeared at Blair's shoulder like a decision. "South boards holding," he said, eyes bright with equal parts fear and clarity. "North ledge has a posting gap."

"How long?"

"Twenty-eight minutes."

"Then it is a failure," Blair said, not cruel, not loud. "Get there. Post the failure first."

He ran, stylus forgotten, chalk held like a relay baton.

The senior auditor saw him go and called after, "We need confirmation!"

"Confirmed by weather," the young one answered over his shoulder.

The corridor's hum dipped to a note that felt like resolve.

Blair climbed toward the east run, where the wall had a history and history loved to repeat itself. The brace there did not groan yet, but it had learned to speak without sound. Ilex joined her, eyes narrowing as he laid a palm to wax.

"Heat drift," he said. "Tiny, but compounding."

He posted: *East Brace: heat variance +2°. Vent half-open. Monitor 10m.*

A gust tested their math. The wall flexed, not dangerously—yet. Blair stared at the board and felt the next hour assemble itself like a plan bearing teeth.

"Make the door board the room," she said. "No adjournments. Everything here."

They dragged a second board beside the first and labeled it East Wall—Live in letters large enough for a frightened body to read at speed.

Pip arrived with a wet grin. "We're making the storm read."

"Let it," Blair said.

Hardliners chose that moment for one last push. Three of them, sashes slick with rain, marched up with a roll of wax paper and a pot of sealant.

"Emergency protocol," their lead declared, voice pitched to be heard over weather. "This corridor will be sealed. Posting will resume after the storm passes. All non-essential personnel will evacuate."

"Define non-essential," Blair said.

"Anyone who writes," he answered, and reached for the first board.

Vetch stepped between sealant and chalk. He didn't bare his teeth; he didn't need to. He simply stood, the way doors stand when they remember their job.

"Posting is essential," Ilex said, almost apologetic in tone, utterly uncompromising in content. "We cannot reinforce what we do not see."

"You will cause panic," the hardliner repeated, as if repetition could turn a slogan into physics.

Sera looked up from a worker's trembling hand. "We cause return," she said, and pointed to the line that said *Return: 2m22.* "That is what rooms are for."

The hardliner shifted tactics, softer and more dangerous. "Then post only to a central slate. Keep the boards dark. We will avoid chaos."

Pip laughed, incredulous. "You think hiding is a sedative. It's a sedition against eyesight."

Blair kept her tone level. "You can stay and help, or you can go and not hinder. Those are the options." She turned to the board. "Write the offer," she told Pip.

Pip chalked it where everyone could see: *Help or don't hinder. Doors stay open.*

The hardliners looked at one another and found no quorum. They left with the sullen dignity of people whose favorite furniture has been rearranged.

The storm deepened.

Wind pressed long, not hard, a pressure meant to unlearn discipline. Water threaded through seams that had sworn they were closed. The hum of the hive lowered another step, into a key no one chose and everyone obeyed.

"East Wall—variance 17%," the young auditor posted, hand steady. "Rising."

"Switch vent to three-quarters," Ilex called, already moving. "Reduce East lanes by one. Rotate load to South. Post returns."

Pip ran the corridor, passing messages even though the board carried them—some orders ask to be carried twice. Sera clipped dew vials to her belt; Vetch held a lane like a shepherd keeps a path through sheep.

A worker stumbled near the brace, eyes blown wide with the kind of fear that thinks in ink, not breath. Sera reached her, palm up. "Consent?"

The worker nodded once, small and immense. Tend in 23 seconds. Return in three minutes, five seconds. The numbers landed on the board like anchors.

"Variance 19%," the auditor posted. "Creeping."

Ilex's jaw tightened. "Torque," he said. "Quarter-turn planned."

He wrote it down—time, intent, reason—because in this hive even fixes arrived with receipts.

"Wait," Blair said, listening to the wall. "On my count." She looked at the board as if the board could look back. "Pip, call the count across the corridors."

Pip's voice carried in a way even wind respected. "Ready on torque—three… two… one—turn."

Ilex turned. The wall sighed. "Variance 17%," the auditor wrote, chalk squeaking as if relieved.

Rain blew sideways, reconsidered, blew backward. Storms change their minds; that is their agency.

A thin crack sounded somewhere above, not at the brace but in the story the brace belonged to. Workers flinched. Fear has muscle memory; it tries to revisit rooms that have been boarded up.

Blair spoke into that memory. "Post," she said. "Every stumble. Every return. Every vent change. If a number slips, write it bigger."

Sable, who had come without fanfare and stood like a shelf, added a small column at the edge: Alarms. He drew three boxes: *wind shift, heat drift, load surge.* When any occurred, he marked a slash in the box. It turned panic into tally and tally into plan.

"Variance 22%," the auditor wrote. "Brace groan audible."

The hardliner from earlier reappeared at the corridor's edge, something like humility stuck in his throat. "What do you need?" he asked Vetch.

"Hands," Vetch said. "Yours."

The man nodded, stepped into a line of six holding a reinforcing span, and found a job that did not require a speech.

Toward midday, the storm found East Wall with something like intent. Wind leaned as if trying to read the numbers while erasing them. Pip kept writing. The chalk looked like bones. The board looked like a ribcage.

"Variance twenty-four," the auditor said, voice steady by force. "Reinforce now."

Ilex had already moved. "Second quarter-turn. On count." He looked to Blair.

"Three," she said. "Two." The wall moaned, the kind of sound that drives prayers out of unbelievers. "One."

They turned. The moan cut off, the way a sob does when breath remembers itself after being held too long. The variance ticked down: *23… 21… 19.* The board recorded it like a pulse settling.

Someone behind them started to clap and stopped, embarrassed. There are times when gratitude feels like disrespect to the work still underway.

Blair exhaled. "Post the throttle on South," she told Ilex. "We owe them capacity."

He nodded, chalked: *South lanes +1. Monitor strain.* Practice made gifts prioritize themselves.

As the storm rolled to its next argument, the corridor found a rhythm grim enough to last: call, post, act, check, care, repeat. The live ledger below the board filled in parallel, ink catching up not days later but minutes. Audit had learned to walk beside the clock. No one celebrated it. That's how you know it's real.

Near dusk—still storm, different temperature—a runner arrived from North Ledge, soaked and breathless. "Our board—" she panted, "washed clean. We can't keep chalk up."

"Post here," Blair said, pointing to a blank section. "You are us while your board dries." She stepped aside so the runner could write. The sentence turned a corridor into a commons.

Sera leaned on the brace for one fraction of a second and closed her eyes. "I can hold," she whispered, as if to the day. "Not forever. Enough."

Pip caught Blair's look. "East Wall?" she asked.

"Not today," Blair said. She meant *not yet.* The wall heard both.

The storm drew a breath the size of the meadow and prepared to push again. The posts stood, wet and stubborn, not pretty, exactly true.

"Tomorrow," Ilex said, reading the wind with the stubbornness of someone who has learned to respect and argue with physics.

"Tonight," Blair corrected gently. "We're not done."

She looked at the board. The board looked like a voice.

"Write," she said.

And they did.

By late afternoon the storm stopped pretending to be weather and began behaving like intent. The wind came in long muscles, not gusts, pressing its argument against East Wall as if it meant to edit the hive out of itself.

The board told the truth faster than mouths. *Variance 20 → 22 → 23.* Ilex posted torque checks; the young auditor mirrored them in the live ledger without looking away from the chalk. Pip refreshed smudged lines with a speed that made the board feel alive. Sera triaged without theater—dew, breath, walk, return—her cadence stubborn as a metronome.

A tremor moved through the brace—small, specific, wrong.

"Hairline," Ilex said, eyes narrow. He didn't touch the crack; he read its posture. "Not load-bearing yet. Can be—if we get stupid."

"Post it," Blair said.

Pip wrote big, as if bigger letters could teach the wall to listen: Hairline at East Brace—monitor—no seal.

The hardliner from earlier reappeared, sealant pot in hand, a last holdout of an old era. "This is the moment," he said, breath harsh with the righteousness fear lends. "We seal, we ride the storm, we sort the rest tomorrow."

Blair didn't raise her voice. "If we seal, we blind. If we blind, we guess. If we guess, we spill." She tapped the line: no seal. "Stay and hold, or go and don't hinder."

He looked at the board. He looked at the hairline. He put the pot down like a habit taught to sit.

Wind leaned harder. Alarms ticked in Sable's small boxes—*wind shift, heat drift, load surge*—slashes like rain made of pencil. The board began to resemble a chest: ribs (braces), breath (returns), pulse (variance), voice (revisions). It was not beautiful. It was irrefutable.

"Variance twenty-four," the auditor wrote. "Creeping."

Ilex ran his palm along wax and listened with a kind of hearing that doesn't live in ears. "Second quarter-turn will help," he said, "but only if we open north vent further. Otherwise we're bracing a pressure we created."

"Do it," Blair said. "Post it. Count it."

Pip's voice again carried: "North vent—three quarter—on my count—three, two, one—turn!"

The wall shuddered, then eased—a long exhale housed in wax. The numbers moved like relief finding its right size: *23… 21.*

Not safe. Safer.

A runner from South arrived, soaked, eyes wide with that private triumph survival lends the sober. "We can take one more lane," she said. "We opened earlier. We're steady."

Blair pointed at a blank patch of board and stepped aside. The runner posted it herself. Truth carries further when written by the hands that earned it.

The storm, offended by their coherence, tried chaos. Rain ricocheted; wind reversed in a fitful eddy; a loose plank somewhere slapped the wall as if to remind them that randomness was on the guest list too. A novice flyer panicked mid-lane, arcing toward the brace.

Vetch intercepted—no grab, just angle—bleeding her momentum into his own and walking her to shade. Sera was there before apology formed. “Consent?” she asked. The novice nodded, embarrassed and brave. *Tend: 17s. Return: 3m02.* Numbers shaved shame down to size.

“Variance twenty-three,” the auditor posted, jaw set. “Holding.”

The senior auditor, who had hovered like a ghost that didn’t know whether it still qualified as living, finally moved. He took a piece of chalk between forefinger and thumb the way one takes a vow. Under the live ledger he wrote, carefully: Ledger synchronized. Board authoritative. He looked at Blair with the expression of a man discovering that humility does not kill.

“Thank you,” Blair said, and meant *welcome back to the present.*

A deep sound rolled under them, not a groan—a note. The kind of note a wall produces to advise you of its childhood.

“Brace origin,” Ilex said. “Where the old patch meets the new.”

He drew a quick diagram at the board’s bottom edge—two circles bridged by a narrow line. Sable, seeing it, smiled in spite of rain. “Bridge symbol,” he murmured. “For crossing places we should not close prematurely.”

“Variance twenty-five,” the auditor posted. His chalk squeaked, the way nerves squeak when told to behave.

“Time for the half-turn?” Pip asked, knowing the answer and asking anyway because ritual becomes useful when it’s honest.

“No,” Ilex said. “We’d snap pride before wax.” He thumbed the torque wrench like a worry stone. “We need distributed help. Six hands. Two spans. Brace the brace.”

Workers stepped forward—no bidding, no picks. The hardliner who had wanted to seal took a place among them. Vetch set their stance. Pip called timing. Sera checked breath like a chorister listening for pitch.

"Count," Blair said.

"Three," Pip called. "Two. One."

They lifted, not heavy, together. The board recorded what bodies did: Aux brace engaged. Load redistributed. Variance slid: *24… 22… 20.*

Somewhere, a lamp guttered and found itself again.

Rain abated by a degree the skin could register. Wind changed its grammar from imperative to interrogative. The storm was not over. But it was bored by their refusal to panic.

A courier from Recovery trotted up, carefully guarding a dry slate beneath his wing. "Care postings continuous," he reported to Sera. "No gaps. Two deferred by consent. Returns tomorrow." He looked proud and tired, which is the right way to look when claiming a day.

"Post it," Sera said.

He did. The board, already crowded, made room. Boards always make room when rooms refuse to.

The young auditor leaned back for the first time in hours and realized his hand cramped. He shook it out, then wrote anyway: Gap log—zero. He underlined it once, then struck the line through and posted a revision: Gap log—zero so far. He circled *so far.*

Sera nodded. "Correction is care for truth."

The senior auditor glanced at the revision column and, to his own surprise, smiled. "I used to think corrections endangered authority," he said to Blair. "Now I see they protect it."

"Authority that doesn't permit correction is theater," Blair said. "Storms don't buy tickets."

The wind took a last hard swipe at East Wall around the hour when bodies believe they have already spent themselves. The brace answered with a sound that made three workers flinch, two pray, and Pip swear once under her breath.

"Variance twenty-six," the auditor posted. "Spiking."

Ilex didn't look at the numbers. He looked at the faces. "We have one more quarter-turn in us," he said quietly. "After that, we're courting vanity. We need a second vent relief. South or West?"

The runner from South, still at the board, tapped her earlier note. "We can stretch," she said. "Not pretty. True."

"West?" Blair asked.

A figure stepped from the crowd no one had seen arrive: the queen, rain darkening her sash to ordinary cloth. "West can give one lane," she said, no fanfare. "They've been posting like a clock that refuses to stop."

"Post it," Blair said.

The queen did not hand the task to a clerk. She wrote it herself—letters plain, the way power writes when it's not performing.

"Count," Pip called, voice hoarse and cheerful. "Three. Two. One."

Wrench. Vent. Span. Breath.

Variance fell: *25… 23… 21.* Like a fever deciding to be memory.

The storm considered this, then moved its attention elsewhere, as storms do when they sense stubbornness.

Someone cried. Not fear. Relief delayed long enough to be trustworthy.

Dusk found the corridor soggy and standing. The board looked like a battlefield map drawn by a pacifist: messy, specific, bleeding information. The live ledger below it matched line for line. No triumphs, just facts. The wall hummed a pitch that suggested the next hour would arrive with nothing catastrophic attached.

Blair checked the revision column, the alarm boxes, the gap log. All the boring instruments of survival glowed with the understated pride of tools put away clean.

Pip leaned her forehead against the cool wax and laughed once. "Windows: 1. Storm: still arguing."

Sera wiped rain off the tend column with two fingers and rewrote a blurred *3m04*. "We will be honest even about the small," she said. "Small becomes big when you ignore it."

The hardliner picked up the sealant pot he had set down and carried it to the tool shelf. "For leaks," he said, not quite meeting anyone's eyes. "Not windows."

Vetch clapped his shoulder, a guard's benediction that conferred membership without ceremony.

The young auditor added a final, almost impolite sentence at the bottom edge of the board, where only those who cleaned up would read it: Ledgers learned to arrive on time today. He looked at the senior auditor, who nodded, a man unbecoming a statue.

Blair looked at the East Wall, at the board, at the faces. "We're not finished," she said, which the corridor heard as permission to stop pretending to be brave for five minutes.

They would eat, they would watch, they would spell each other at the board through the night. The storm would have more to say in the hours when lamps dim, and doubt speaks in familiar voices. But the wall had learned a new word: *now*.

And now, for the first time that day, felt like enough.

Night rubbed the edges off the hive, turning corridors into outlines and faces into voices. Lamps guttered; wicks learned patience. Rain slowed to an argument with itself. Wind, bored of shouting, began to test for whispering failures—drafts at seams, loosened pins, habits that break when no one is watching.

The board did not sleep. It shone like a square of moon hammered to a wall. Chalk lines dulled to gray, then brightened wherever a fresh hand retraced them. The live ledger beneath it drank the same facts in slower strokes, ink gathering them into a memory that would not forget.

Blair set the watch in pairs: one to read, one to act. Pip took first with Vetch. Sera lay down for 20 minutes that lasted twelve. Ilex paced the length of the brace as if walking a boundary he meant to keep.

"Variance nineteen," the young auditor posted, shoulders uneven with fatigue. "Holding."

"Vent check at quarter," Pip answered, writing it before she spoke it so the sound wouldn't have to carry responsibility alone. Vetch moved to the lever like a rumor you can trust.

From the dimmer corridors came small requests that told the truth about solidarity: *Borrow chalk? Post here while our board dries? Confirm our tend time—my hands shook.* The East Wall board made room each time, the way a good room shifts its furniture to hold more chairs.

A stray gust found a loose plank above the brace. It slapped once, a wet palm against wax. Ilex's head snapped up. "Hear that?"

"Not the brace," Vetch said, listening with his shoulders.

"Not yet," Ilex replied, already chalking: Loose plank above brace—inspect—no load. He took two steps up the ladder and pressed his palm flat. The plank muttered once, then consented to a wedge. The board got another line: Secured.

The queen appeared out of darkness the way morning decisions do: gently, as if they'd been up all night thinking without announcing it. Her sash was soaked to the color of work cloth. She said nothing. She took up a cloth and wiped the revision column clean where rain had smudged a digit, then waited for the next correction and wrote it herself.

"Your hands will be quoted," Sable murmured, half a smile in the lamplight.

"I prefer my hands to be useful," she answered, and added a small check beside Gap log—0 so far as if blessing boredom.

Near midnight, weather remembered cruelty. A wind shear sliced across the east run, thinner than earlier blasts but sharper, like a question someone asks to make you slip. The brace sang a high, mean note. Three workers flinched; one froze.

Sera was there, quiet as a glove. "Consent?" she asked. The worker's eyes fluttered. "Yes," she whispered, and breath became hers again.

"Variance twenty-one," the auditor posted. "Spike transient."

Pip leaned into the board with a stub of chalk that had performed beyond its lifespan. "Transient is still strain," she wrote. "Vent two clicks."

"Wait," Ilex said. He touched the wax, not tenderly, respectfully. "Two clicks will overshoot. One and a half."

"You can write halves?" Pip teased without smiling and wrote 1½ like a small rebellion against integers.

"Count," Blair said.

They turned the lever as if it were a sentence in need of a better verb. The pitch settled. The board logged the new number with a satisfaction that did not dare relax.

The hardliner—the same one who'd retired his sealant—brought tea that tasted like survival and set it without comment by the ledger. He met Blair's eye for one second, and in that second an old allegiance found a new job.

In the deep hours, light went thin and time fat. The board showed nothing dramatic, which felt like sacrilege given the theater storms prefer. Vetch took second watch with Sera; Pip dozed upright against the brace with her twine coiled around a finger like a promise.

"Variance eighteen," the auditor wrote. "Holding." He added so far without being told.

Sera checked the tend column, rubbed away a smudge, and re-inked 3m04 from memory. "Small kept small," she said softly, proud of a plain fact.

A runner from North Ledge stumbled in, breath misting in a thread. "We're steady," she reported. "But our board cracked. Writing on the wall now, direct." She grinned, teeth bright in the dark. "Turns out walls can be windows if you shame them into it."

"Post that," Sable said, and when she hesitated, No, the sentence." She wrote: Walls can be windows if you shame them into it. The board accepted philosophy at 2:13 a.m. and did not appear to mind.

The queen leaned toward the alarm boxes and drew a neat slash in *heat drift*. "Two degrees," she said, unhurried. "We can afford it."

"We can also post it," Blair replied.

They posted both.

The near miss came at the hour when ink blots look like omens. A drone delivering a late brace pin misread a gesture and set the pin against a seam in the wrong direction—nothing catastrophic, but badly timed. The plank above the brace jittered, knocking the wedge loose. Fear moved faster than physics; three bodies reached for the wrong thing.

"Stop," Ilex said, the word not sharp, simply final. He set the pin correctly, reset the wedge, then looked at the board and wrote: Almost mistake—pin reversed by fatigue. He placed it in the revision column, then copied it line-for-line into the live ledger.

The queen watched his hand. "You just posted a near-failure."

"Near-failures teach cheaper," Ilex said. "If we let them."

Blair added a line under his: Alarm check—night shift extra glance at pins. Pip underlined *extra* so hard the chalk broke.

Vetch positioned a stool beneath the plank, not to hold, to invite attention. It felt like teaching the wall to raise its hand before speaking.

"Variance nineteen," the auditor posted, calmer. "Recovering."

Sera pressed dew into her own temples. "I can hold," she told nobody. The sentence had become her prayer.

Toward false dawn, the storm exhausted its verbs. Rain descended to drizzle; wind decided to speak to other walls. The hum of the hive rose a note, like breath after coughing.

"East: seventeen," the auditor wrote. He capped his chalk as if tucking a child in. "Gap log—0. Revisions—5. Alarms—7. Returns posted—32."

"Ledger matches," the senior auditor said, and the words did not sound like surrender anymore; they sounded like teamwork.

The queen made one final entry, in a neat small hand at the board's bottom edge: Windows intact. Doors open. Clocks kept. She did not sign it. Authority, having learned something, sometimes leaves itself out of the sentence.

Light bled into the corridor with the caution of someone entering a room where grief might be sleeping. It found none—only fatigue arranged into usefulness.

Workers drifted in twos and threes, drawn by the rumor of morning. They touched the board like a relic and found, to their relief, that it was only wood and chalk and their own handwriting. Some smiled; some cried a little as if their faces remembered a different storm and were surprised to survive this one.

Pip unwound the twine from her finger and tied a new knot at *five and a half* seconds—no one's rule, everyone's dare. "Alarm check," she told a yawning novice, half joke, all instruction. The novice nodded solemnly, as if being sworn in.

Ilex noted torque with the relish of a man who prefers numbers to naps. Vetch stretched his back in a way that made his armor look like posture instead of metal. Sera tucked an empty dew vial into a pocket and patted it like a pet that had done good work.

Blair stood very still and let the corridor's ordinariness arrive. It came shyly, then claimed the place. She turned to the board and ran a fingertip down the revision column, then across the gap log, then through the alarm boxes where slashes had started to look like tally marks on the inside of a jail a day before release. She breathed out the sentence the day had been trying to write through them:

> "We stayed present." It wasn't poetry. It was maintenance.

The queen closed the ledger with two hands. "Storms do not grade courage," she said. "They grade practice. We passed enough to earn another day." She looked at Blair. "Make it dull."

"Dull and on time," Blair said, as if promising breakfast.

They dispersed to sweep water, reset vents, replace stubbed chalk with longer sticks. The board kept glowing, not brighter—truer. Outside, the meadow tried on the color called morning and found it fit.

The storm had not apologized. It had simply left. Windows still stood. Hinges had learned a new sound. Clocks had not stopped.

Pip caught Blair's shoulder. "Is the chapter done?" she asked, exhausted, hopeful.

"Chapters don't end on storms," Blair said gently. "They end on what you do after."

Pip grinned the grin of someone who has already started.

Morning wore the hive like a bandage: snug, a little tender, holding. Water pooled in polite corners. The East Wall breathed slower. Workers stepped carefully, as if not to wake a sleeping bruise.

The board was a palimpsest of endurance—chalk softened by damp, revisions tucked like sutures, alarm boxes crossed with slashes that looked less like panic now and more like arithmetic. The live ledger beneath it matched line for line, ink drying into memory.

"Gap log—zero," the young auditor read, voice rough with use. He underlined *zero* once, lightly, like the opposite of a victory lap. "Revisions: five. Alarms: seven. Returns posted: thirty-two. Spills: nil."

"Check the torque," Ilex said, because that was the counter-spell to speechifying.

He did, posted, nodded. "Stable."

Sera moved along the corridor with a cloth, not to polish—polish was for mirrors—but to clear the board where smears could confuse a tired eye. She rewrote three digits and added one small word beside them: clear.

Pip distributed fresh sticks of chalk as if handing out bread. To a novice she said, "Alarm check?" The novice pointed at the boxes and grinned. "Wind shift," she said solemnly, "heat drift, load surge." She drew a tentative slash through *heat drift* for the minor rise the ledger already noted. The board accepted the hand of the new as casually as it had accepted the hands of the old.

Vetch repositioned a stool, checked a latch, lifted an empty bucket. Guards in this hive did not retire when storms did; they tidied.

Blair let the ordinariness dwell. She checked the revision column one last time and saw it had stopped craving attention. That was how she knew they could afford speeches.

The queen called the gathering at midday. No dais, no banners. The corridor where East Wall had argued all night became a hall by consensus. Workers stood with wet ankles and dry eyes. The boards lined the wall like a new alphabet that had finally learned its sounds.

"Storms do not flatter," the queen began, voice even and near. "They do not applaud windows or punish mirrors. They simply measure your practice in their own units."

She gestured to the board. "We kept clocks. We posted returns. We corrected in light. We wrote 'so far' when honesty required humility. We refused to seal a bell to a wall." Her mouth tilted, almost a smile. "We learned to write halves."

A ripple of tired laughter moved through the room, affectionate as a nudge.

"From this day," she continued, "*The Ledger and the Clock* governs storms. Not as suggestion—law. Door boards must remain visible; gaps are to be posted in the minute; revisions welcome; ledgers parallel, not prior. Guards will protect posting. Risk will stand at doors. Audit will arrive with chalk first, ink second. And any who try to turn windows into ornaments will answer for delay, not for insolence."

She touched the board with two fingers and left no signature. "We passed enough to earn another day. Let us make that day dull."

It was the right sermon because it didn't want to be one.

Refugees from the north moved through the crowd like exhalations that had finally found air. Their wings were a little torn, their voices a little careful.

Pip led them to the board, not to the cell assignments. "Write your names," she said, tapping an open strip along the bottom edge. "Then write one practice you can carry." She pointed to her own: Pip—alarm check with a neat knot drawn beside it.

A tall flyer with a scar at his ridge wrote Kerr—tend in time and then hesitated. "We were punished for writing," he confessed.

"Here," Sera said gently, "you will be punished for *not* posting."

He laughed once, incredulity turning into a cough that resembled relief. He logged two small returns before the meeting ended, hands shaking less each time.

A young clerk from the fallen hive—eyes like damp ash—hovered by the live ledger. The senior auditor stepped aside. "Ink after chalk," he said, and placed a stylus in her hand as if returning a stolen season. She copied a line carefully: Variance 17 → 16 (vent ½). She exhaled like a door that had stuck, then moved.

Sable added a new page to the archive labeled *Guests' Hands* and wrote a rule at the top in tiny script: No attribution without consent.

Names written by the writer, not by the archive. He underlined *consent* twice, as if to anchor it with a nail that had learned subtlety.

In the afternoon, the Outcomes Board performed the least photogenic ritual in the hive: a reconciliation walk. They moved from board to ledger to wall to vent to brace to faces, confirming nothing dramatic, correcting two tiny transpositions, and praising exactly once—when a novice rewrote a blurred *3m04* without being asked.

"Boring," the senior officer said afterward, pleased as a mason with straight mortar. "Keep it."

Enablement arrived late, carrying a tasteful proposal and a sheepish smile. "We can design a storm dashboard," their lead offered. "Minimalist. Elegant."

Blair shook her head. "Storms don't read dashboards. They read hinges. If you must, build a one-page checklist. Print it ugly."

The lead nodded, oddly relieved to be spared the burden of elegance. "Ugly is cheaper," she murmured, and went to find a piece of ugly wax.

Ilex rolled out a new schedule beneath *The Ledger & the Clock—v1: Quarter-turn audit weekly, live post at shift open/mid/close, rotation plan pre-storm, cross-post permission.* He added a line at the bottom: If another hive arrives, treat their boards as ours until theirs stand.

"Export without conquest," Reeve said, appearing with his unhandsome objectivity. "We will share clocks. Not banners."

"Share alarms," Pip added, tapping her knot.

"Share corrections," Sera said, tapping the revision column.

"Share dullness," Blair finished. The room accepted it, because dullness had just saved a wall.

Near dusk, a new sound joined the hum: cautious tapping from the edge of the meadow. Scouts. The refugees had sent a signal in return—two short, one long—an agreement to a code no one had to own to obey. The hive answered with three steady taps—their posted availability, their promise to share.

"Windows travel," the queen said quietly, standing beside Blair as light flattened into evening. "We will be judged by how we send them."

"Ladders, not banners," Blair replied.

"And clocks," the queen said. "Clocks that anyone can wind."

They watched the meadow darken with a calm that felt earned, not promised.

That night, the archive breathed like a bakery after closing—warm, orderly, smelling faintly of sugar and work. Sable filed *Storm Day—East Wall* beside *Window Standard* and *Rooms With Locks*. He tucked into the folder a stub of chalk, a broken knot of twine, and a scrap of cloth the queen had used to clean the revision column. Archives cannot save a hive, but they can keep it from forgetting what and how it learned.

Kel—steady now, carrying real load—stopped at the threshold and wrote a line low on the board where only sweepers would see it in the morning: They measured my flight today. Not my silence. He didn't sign. The hive knew his handwriting.

Vetch took last watch. He stood not like a statue and not like a guard who expects trouble, but like a door. When a stray draft found the seam again, he put a shoulder to it, not to block air, to remind wood of its job.

Sera slept the kind of sleep that returns you intact. Ilex dreamed of torque and woke grinning, because only carpenters consider that a treat. Pip coiled her twine and tucked it under the board, a private superstition that had accidentally become policy. The young auditor set his chalk beside the ink without hierarchy.

Blair remained a moment longer, alone. She placed the open circle and the ladder token at the edge of the board, then added the tiniest mark—a dot next to *alarm*. Not an exclamation, not a warning. A readiness. She looked at the wall and felt it look back with the bored kindness of a house that has learned its weight again.

The storm had done its job. It had graded practice. Practice had passed.

From the meadow's edge, the faintest pattern of far taps drifted in—call-and-answer, distant and insistent. Other hives were listening. Some would ask to borrow windows; some would try to rename them; some would come to test them.

Pip appeared at Blair's side, hair damp, eyes bright with a fatigue that flirts with joy. "Is the morning ours?" she asked.

"It's everyone's," Blair said. "That's the point."

She nodded toward the boards, toward the ledger, toward the wall. "Tomorrow we show them how to watch."

And the hum rose, thin at first, then wide—the sound a house makes when it chooses not to hide.

8
Hives Watching

Storms do not end when the rain stops. They linger in wings, in joints, in the way bees glance at braces as if expecting sound. And they linger in rumor, which travels faster than wind.

By the second morning, scouts returned not with weather reports but with questions: other hives had heard. Messengers carried fragments—*a hive that posted in chalk during the storm, a queen who wrote corrections herself, a wall that bent but did not fall because workers counted in time instead of ceremony.*

The meadow became a waiting room. Delegations landed by the dozen: wings still wet from their own weather, voices carrying accents of fear. They wanted to see the boards. They wanted to touch the chalk. Some wanted to steal it, others to sanctify it.

The queen convened the hive in the central corridor. This time she stood with Blair, Sera, Ilex, Pip, Vetch, and the auditors at her side—not above, but level. Behind them, door boards leaned in a row like a makeshift choir: Recovery, Risk, Audit, Storm Day. The chalk lines had been refreshed but not polished; their mess was the proof.

"Hives are watching," the queen said. "Some will come to learn. Some to doubt. Some to claim. We will open, but we will not bend to flattery or fear."

She looked at Blair. "Show them what windows mean."

Blair nodded, heart tight. The next chapter would not be written only by their hive. It would be read by others, and reading always edits the text.

The first visitors came from a hive to the west, sleek and orderly. Their leader introduced himself with a bow so low it seemed practiced.

"We admire your resilience," he said. "We request your method—codified, sealed, transferable. We will adopt it as a framework across our chambers."

DOI: 10.1201/9781003740056-8

Pip frowned. "Framework? It's not a banner."

"Not banner," the leader insisted. "Assurance. We will call it *Resilient Hive Model*™."

The trademark hung in the air like a shutter nailed to daylight.

Ilex shook his head. "Storms do not respect models. They respect torque. Postings. Schedules."

Sera added, "And consent. Do you plan to export consent?"

The leader hesitated. "Consent complicates adoption."

Blair stepped forward. "Then you will export nothing but mirrors. Keep your banners. Windows do not survive when carried as trophies."

The delegation left with tight smiles, murmuring about refinement. Their notes looked like seals in waiting.

The next delegation came from the south, smaller, wings frayed. Their leader—a worker, not a queen—spoke plainly.

"We lost half our honey last season. Our braces sagged. Our auditors posted late. We heard you survived. Will you teach us?"

Sera guided them to the Recovery board. "Write," she said, handing chalk. "Not a speech. Write your last tend time."

A young flyer stepped forward, hand trembling, and scrawled: Tend 2m11. Return 9m. Spill: yes.

Pip erased nothing. She wrote beneath: Tend target: <30s. Return: <5m. Spill: preventable. She circled the words.

The visitors touched the chalk as if it were warm. "We can try," one whispered.

"Not try," Vetch said. "Practice. Storms don't grade effort."

The delegation nodded, relief visible. They asked for no banners, only schedules. Those could travel.

By afternoon, another group arrived—northern, the same direction the refugees had come. Their queen walked at the center, her crown bright but her eyes brittle. She examined the boards with disdain disguised as curiosity.

"You survived because your storm was mild," she declared. "Our hive faces harsher winds. Chalk and boards are children's toys."

Pip bristled. "Toys don't hold walls."

The northern queen waved a dismissive wing. "We prefer discipline. Silence. Our workers endure without posting their shame on walls."

"Your workers are silent because they are gone," one of the refugees muttered, unable to contain himself.

The queen's eyes sharpened, but she said nothing. She left with her retinue, her silence heavier than any decree.

Blair watched her go and felt the edge of the mentor's warning: storms reveal whether your braces were practice or posture. That queen's silence was posture, and posture breaks.

At dusk, the archive filled with questions written by outsiders:

- *How do you enforce posting?*
- *What if workers lie?*
- *How do you punish delay?*
- *What happens when the queen disagrees?*

Sable pinned them under a heading: Questions Carried In. Beneath, he added: Answers Must Be Posted, Not Promised.

Blair studied the board. Some questions were earnest, some predatory. She remembered the mentor's counsel: *send ladders, not banners.*

"Write one page," she told Ilex, Sera, and Pip. "Plain. Ugly. No slogans. Essentials only."

They drafted through the evening:

- Essentials first. Latch, wings, weather.
- Care in time. Tend <30s. Return <5m. Post always.
- Outcomes only. Spills, strain, outputs. Numbers, not names.
- Consent governs. Care deferred until yes.
- Boards at doors. Gaps logged. Revisions welcome.
- Ledger parallel. Ink after chalk. Never before.
- Guards protect posting. Windows stay open.

Sable copied it clean, then left wide margins labeled *for storms.*

"This is what we export," Blair said. "Not models. Not frameworks. Practice."

The meadow swarmed with watching eyes. Some hives circled, cautious, measuring distance. Some hovered, ready to pounce or plead. The storm had passed, but a larger storm—the kind made of envy, fear, and ambition—was gathering.

Pip whispered to Blair at the threshold, "We survived the storm. Now we must survive being seen."

Blair nodded, watching the shadows of other hives lengthen across the grass. "And being copied," she said. "Which may be the harsher test."

The hum of their hive deepened, readying itself. Windows had held against wind. Now they would have to hold against interpretation.

By the second day, the meadow looked like a marketplace of meanings. Hives sent scouts, envoys, agitators—each with a different interpretation of what they thought they had seen.

One delegation arrived with banners already printed. Their leader, a wax-polished strategist, unfurled a cloth covered in diagrams. "We call it the Window Excellence Framework," he announced proudly. "Four tiers of champions, three councils of oversight, monthly pageants of care."

Pip gagged audibly. "Pageants?"

"Visibility inspires discipline," the leader explained. "If care becomes spectacle, compliance follows."

Sera shook her head. "Care is not theater. It is time. The more you dress it up, the more you slow it down."

The strategist frowned. "Workers need recognition."

"Workers need return," Sera corrected. She pointed to the Recovery board. "These numbers kept wings aloft. Where are your numbers?"

The strategist shuffled, muttered about "phased implementation," and left in a swirl of fabric that already looked heavier than any brace could carry.

Later, a different hive arrived—lean, stern, wings clipped short as a mark of rank. Their envoy sneered at the boards. "Chalk is too easy to falsify," he said. "We demand metal tablets, stamped with seals, witnessed by three overseers. Anything less is corruption."

Ilex stepped forward, grime still on his fingers from torque checks. "Storms do not wait for seals. They wait for nothing. Chalk may smear, but chalk is instant. Metal is vanity."

The envoy's lip curled. "We value integrity over speed."

"Then you value corpses over corrections," Ilex replied. "Storms don't ask if your ledger shines. They ask if your brace holds."

The envoy stalked away, wings stiff, muttering about "recklessness."

Blair turned to her circle. "Every hive wants to translate windows into its own dialect. But the dialect doesn't matter. Practice does."

In the archive that evening, the boards carried new graffiti from visitors:

- *Our leaders will never allow corrections—how did you convince yours?*
- *If chalk smears, how do you prove it happened?*
- *What if our queen forbids windows?*

Sable pinned them with his usual calm. "Questions worth keeping," he said. "Answers must live in practice, not in speeches."

Blair studied the lines. Some were hungry, others manipulative. She knew which kind would survive storms.

"Teach only what can survive boredom," she said finally. "If they want drama, let them build banners. If they want dullness, give them chalk."

On the third morning, the northern queen returned, this time with twice as many attendants. She walked the corridor like a prosecutor.

"These boards are chaos," she declared. "Numbers smeared. Lines crooked. Workers scribbling without permission. How can you call this truth?"

Blair gestured to the live ledger beneath. "Because truth matches. Chalk and ink. Immediate and record. Parallel, not prior."

The queen scoffed. "You confuse mess with honesty."

"No," Pip said, stepping forward, twine still looped at her wrist. "We confuse honesty with survival. And survival is always messy."

The northern queen's attendants bristled, but she lifted a wing to quiet them. "Your hive will fall," she said coldly. "Storms respect order, not graffiti."

"Then why did your walls break first?" one of the refugees asked from the back. His voice carried because silence had trained him too long.

The queen's jaw clenched. She turned sharply and left, her crown catching light that refused to flatter.

That evening, Blair walked to the meadow, heart heavy. The mentor appeared, wings flecked with distant dust.

"They twist what they see," Blair said. "Some call it theater, some call it corruption. How do we keep windows from becoming ornaments?"

The figure tilted its head. "You cannot prevent twisting. You can only practice until twisting looks foolish."

Blair frowned. "But they have louder voices."

"Storms are louder still," the mentor said. "Storms will correct lies. Your task is to keep your practice alive until storms arrive. Then truth will side with those who measure while it matters."

Blair exhaled. "So we endure their noise."

"You post your numbers," the figure corrected. "Noise hates numbers."

It vanished, leaving the meadow full of evening hum.

The next delegation surprised them. It wasn't queens or envoys—it was workers, sneaking out from a hive in the east. Their wings were frayed, their eyes cautious.

"We've been told windows are dangerous," one said quietly. "That boards invite blame. But we saw your storm logs. Can you… show us how to write?"

Pip pressed chalk into her palm. "Not how. Just do."

The worker hesitated, then scrawled: Tend 1m47. Return 6m12. Spill: yes. She flinched as if expecting punishment. None came. Only nods.

"Now revise," Sera said gently. "Write what would have helped."

The worker added: Tend target <30s. Return target <5m. Need: faster dew.

She stared at the words, tears running tracks down her face. "We were told truth must be signed by three overseers."

Blair shook her head. "Truth must be lived in time. Overseers can stamp after, but they cannot stamp breath."

The workers exchanged looks that smelled like rebellion. They left at dusk, chalk smudges on their fingers, walking straighter than they had arrived.

As darkness fell, the hive hummed with tension. They had survived storms of weather. Now they faced storms of interpretation.

Blair stood at the threshold, watching shadows of distant hives flicker against the meadow. Some shadows leaned close, curious. Others leaned away, calculating.

"Storms outside test braces," she whispered. "Storms between hives test meaning."

Pip joined her, eyes sharp. "Then we post meaning too. One board, one page, one practice. Ugly, boring, true."

Blair nodded. "And let storms—natural or political—decide who was honest."

The boards behind them glowed under lamplight, messy, stubborn, alive.

By the fourth morning, the meadow learned a new chore: diplomacy. Runners carried notes between hives like bees ferrying pollen that might be poison or cure. Some messages arrived folded neat as uniforms; others were creased from being hidden in feathers. The door boards kept working while the hive learned to read letters without forgetting numbers.

The first alliance offered itself with flattery. A midsize hive to the southwest proposed a pact: shared scouts, mutual aid, and an "Innovation Summit" to showcase windows. Their queen wrote in the language of invitations that expect applause.

"Summits are mirrors," Pip said, reading over Blair's shoulder.

"Mutual aid is a door," Ilex countered.

Sera tapped the part that mattered. "'During storms, we will cross-post outcomes across hives so that gaps do not become deaths.' That line can live. The rest can dress itself or not."

Blair folded the letter until only that sentence showed, then brought it to the queen. "We can sign a sentence," she said. "Not a summit."

The queen agreed with an economy that felt like gratitude. "Sign the sentence. Leave the stage to those who need it."

They posted the pact at the door under Cross-Posting in Storms and left blank space beneath labeled *who else?* The blank filled by dusk.

Rumors began to travel faster than agreements. A whisper grew legs: *The hive with boards had formed a window cult.* The phrase spread, sticky as honey spilled on the wrong day. It wore different outfits depending on who told it: sometimes threatening, sometimes ridiculous, always useful to those who preferred mirrors.

A delegation from the east arrived bristling with judgment. Their envoy cleared his throat the way men do before saying a practiced insult. "We hear you punish those who refuse to write," he said.

"We protect those who do," Vetch answered, and planted himself like a short sentence with long meaning.

"You shame mistakes publicly," the envoy insisted.

"We correct them publicly," Sera said. "Shame is private. Practice is not."

“Your workers worship numbers,” he pressed.

“Our workers use numbers,” Ilex said. “They prefer survival to worship.”

The envoy left muttering about zealotry. He didn’t notice a visiting worker copy Tend <30s into her palm and carry it away like a talisman that breathed.

Late afternoon brought a gentler attempt at alliance: a compact hive to the south whose queen had the eyes of someone who had flown lanes. She spoke without assistants.

“Your windows saved you,” she said, “but our council loves frameworks. Give them a ladder, not a sermon?”

Blair smiled despite fatigue. “We have one page,” she said, and handed over the ugly sheet Sable had copied with wide margins for storms. “It’s not a framework. It’s furniture.”

The southern queen read it once, lips moving as if fitting the words to her rhythm. “We will post this at our doors,” she said. “If our council asks for a crest, we will draw a small clock and tell them it is a halo.”

Pip grinned. “Invite us to your storm,” she said. “We’ll post with you.”

“Invite us to yours,” the queen returned. “And we’ll bring ugly wax.”

They clasped wrists—no treaty scroll, just skin that had learned work.

The northern queen returned again, this time with a rumor as weapon. She claimed their hive had adopted “immediate ledgers,” thicker and grander than chalk, stamped in real time by three overseers and a priest.

“Chalk is for children,” she said. “We have invented adult speed.”

Blair didn’t argue. She asked a question windows love. “Where do you post?”

“In the sanctum,” the queen replied, pleased.

“Who can see?”

“Authorized readers,” she said, and the words folded in on themselves like damp paper.

“Then your ledgers are mirrors,” Blair said, still gentle. “They reflect the faces of the authorized.”

Pip folded her arms. “Storms don’t carry badges.”

The northern queen turned on her heel. Her crown shone the way oil does just before it makes you slip.

That evening the queen summoned Blair to the small room where agreements begin. The room had no banners, only a table, a box of chalk, and a ledger open to a page labeled *what we will not forget.*

"Others will keep arriving," the queen said. "Some to learn; some to harvest; some to prosecute. We must decide what we can share, and what we cannot let leave these walls without breaking."

Blair sat, hands restless. "We can share schedules. Post intervals. Consent rules. Tend and return targets. Gap logging, revision columns, live ledger parallel. The dull spine."

"And what can we not?" the queen pressed.

"Us," Blair said. "Our posture. Our refusal to name heroes. Our habit of letting corrections stand. Our way of guarding posting without turning guards into priests. The tone. If we export that, it becomes creed."

The queen nodded, slow approval. "So: ladders, not banners. Tools, not titles."

"And alarms," Blair added. "Teach them to ring for anyone. If clocks are generous, envy dies faster."

The queen closed the ledger as if approving an invoice. "Write *Shareable* and *Non-Shareable* on a page the meadow can read."

Blair did: Shareable: one-pagers, schedules, checklists, cross-posting, live ledger, gap logs, revision practice, consent lines, door boards, guard charter. Non-Shareable: authority by charisma, pageants, champions, medals, secrecy rules, any blessing that costs speed, any doctrine that forbids correction, the right to dominate another hive with our story.

Sable copied it to an ugly wax and posted it under What Travels. Pip added a smaller card beside it: What Doesn't: *our pride.* She drew a tiny ladder and a smaller halo mislabeled clock.

The hive laughed in the way houses do when relieved to find their furniture still fits.

Attempts at distortion didn't stop; they became more inventive. A visiting strategist announced a three-step "Window Pledge" for workers to recite each morning. "Repetition builds culture," he said.

"Repetition builds calluses," Sera replied. "We need blood flow."

The strategist tried a different angle: "At least allow a quarterly Window Gala to celebrate your best postings."

"Gala?" Pip blinked. "For chalk?"

Ilex slid a slate forward, a single number written in thick hand: 0 spills (storm day). "Here's our gala," he said. "Take a picture."

They did not.

That night (because hives like to test agreements when lamps are low), a pair of envoys cornered Blair at the threshold with a contract that smelled like perfume and intimidation. "Exclusive partnership," they said. "Your *Ledger & Clock* becomes our brand. We distribute. You approve."

Blair stared at the phrase *exclusive partnership* until ink stopped pretending to be language. "No," she said.

"You'll reach more hives," they coaxed.

"We'll reach fewer truths," Blair said. "Windows are not franchises."

They left offended by a refusal that didn't bother to rise in volume. Vetch watched them go with the contentment of a door that has just remembered it locks from the inside.

The next morning, the queen gathered the circle with a brief agenda: two minutes of talk, an hour of practice. "Define your field kit," she said. "When we send teams to other hives, what travels in their pockets?"

They emptied the table like a hand revealing its cards:

- One-page Ledger & Clock (ugly, with margins).
- Chalk and stylus (both, without hierarchy).
- Twine with knots (Pip's, copied—a portable cadence for tend time).
- Dew vial (not metaphorical).
- Guard card (Vetch's charter: *protect posting, not prestige*).
- Consent slips (Sera's design: one word, *yes* or *not yet*).
- Gap log slate (pre-ruled, with the word so far printed at the top).

"That is a rescue kit," Reeve said from the doorway, uninvited and welcome. "It doesn't require permission to start. Good."

"Add a sentence," Sable suggested, dipping his stylus. "One that carries posture without prescribing it." He wrote, Windows are for seeing, not posing. He circled *seeing* once, softly.

The queen approved with a nod that felt like a green light set to *dull.*

By late day, a partnership proposal arrived that smelled different: practical, under-signed, no crest. Three small hives proposed a mutual *Gap Watch*: during storms, whichever hive had the least strain would host the others' postings, eyes-on for gaps. No one would command; everyone would count.

Blair looked at Ilex. He smiled, a carpenter's smile. "That's load distribution for truth," he said. "Say yes."

They posted the *Gap Watch* beside *Cross-Posting in Storms.* The board grew another column labeled neighbors. Names went up. Not councils. Names.

The northern queen's rumor machine sputtered. It had nothing to eat but pride and the weather had taken that diet away.

At twilight, Blair found the meadow quiet for the first time in a week. The mentor appeared like a habit she had built, not a ritual she performed.

"They will keep twisting," Blair said. "We will keep posting. Does practice win?"

"Sometimes," the figure said. "When boredom is braced. When dullness is defended. When ladders are shared without demanding your hymn be sung."

Blair smiled, an expression earned by sweat, not plot. "We have a field kit."

"Good," the mentor said. "Now teach without becoming teachers."

"How?"

"Ask them to write before they speak," it said. "Storms don't remember speeches. They remember numbers."

It vanished, leaving a path of air that smelled faintly like pencils.

Blair turned toward the hive and the waiting boards. Tomorrow they would send a team to the southern queen, and another would arrive with a rumor disguised as help, and someone would try to name a dashboard after a mirror. The door boards would not care. They would keep asking for chalk.

And the meadow, which grades hives the way weather does—without agenda—kept watching.

By week's end, rumor discovered rhythm. *Window cult* became chorus, sung off-key across the meadow. The tune changed by hive but kept the same hook: *They worship boards. They punish doubt. They measure love by chalk.* It was lazy music, and lazy music travels.

The misinformation moved like mist—hard to point at, easy to breathe. Refugees flinched when they posted. Visiting workers paused at the revision column as if it might bite. Two delegates arrived carrying pamphlets with mirrors printed on the cover and the title *Objectivity, Not Obsession.*

Vetch read a page, snorted, and used it to shim a wobbly stool. The stool steadied. "Best use yet," he said.

The queen did not call for denunciations. She called for a forum, public and plain, where questions would be asked and answered while hands worked. "Noise hates numbers," she said. "Let noise sit in a room with a clock."

They posted the time on a door board. They added a line beneath: Bring questions. Bring chalk.

The forum filled without being grand. No dais. Two long tables, one with dew and twine and chalk, the other with ledgers and slates. Windows open. Weather undecided. Delegations ranged along the walls: sleek crowns, frayed wings, curious clerks, agitated envoys. The northern queen's attendants arrived crisp as leaf edges. The southern queen stood at the back with workers at her elbow.

The queen opened with a sentence the hive had learned to trust: "We will show before we say." She nodded to Blair.

Blair beckoned a volunteer—Kel, steady now—to simulate a stumble. He launched, wobbled on cue, landed by Sera. "Tend," Sera said, and did. "Return," Kel said, and did. Pip posted: Tend 21s. Return 3m09. The young auditor logged it in the live ledger. Ilex pointed to the vents and made a half-click adjustment just to prove a board could hold more than bodies. The wall did not care; it held.

"Questions?" Blair asked.

An envoy raised a pamphlet like a shield. "How do you ensure accuracy? Chalk can lie."

"Revision column," Sera said, tapping it. Pip added a correction no one needed, small and specific: 21s → 22s (timer lag). She signed it with a dot, not a name. The ledger mirrored the change. "Accuracy is not a freeze," Sera added. "It's a posture."

A clerk with honest worry asked, "What if workers refuse to post because they fear blame?"

"Consent governs care," Blair answered. "But posting is governance. If a corridor won't post, anyone may post in its place. Guards will protect the posting. We punish delay, not doubt."

A polished strategist smirked. "You've replaced rituals with... busyness. How do we know it matters?"

"Storm grades," Ilex said, touching the East Wall board. "Results, not rhetoric."

A northern attendant thrust forward. "You shame mistakes."

Pip shook her head. "We correct them." She wrote a fresh line: Almost mistake—pin reversed. She underlined *almost.* The room, forced to look at a near-failure without drama, felt the strange relief of honesty that refused to blush.

The envoy from *Objectivity, Not Obsession* tried a final gambit. "If numbers rule, where is love?"

Sera smiled with the patience of someone who knows the answer is older than the question. "Love is why we post in time."

A murmur rose—not applause, not outrage. Something more durable: comprehension inching forward.

The queen stepped to the board with an ugly wax sheet in hand—the *Shareable/Non-Shareable* compact Sable had copied in thick strokes. She pinned it beside *Cross-Posting in Storms* and read aloud, not for poetry but for memory.

"Shareable: one-page schedules, tend/return targets, consent lines, door boards, live ledger in parallel, gap logs with *so far,* revision practice, guard charter to protect posting, cross-posting during storms.

Non-Shareable: titles that slow care, pageants, champions, medals, secrecy rules, blessings that cost speed, doctrines that forbid correction, the right to dominate another hive with our story."

She turned to the room. "We will give the first list freely. We will defend the second list from export. Not because we are precious, but because when tone travels, it turns to creed. Creeds become mirrors."

The southern queen nodded. The northern attendants bristled. A compact hive near the door wrote *so far* in their own script on their own slate, and it looked right.

"Now," the queen added, "we do one more thing: show how *Shareable* behaves when it meets weather."

They ran a live drill, not a pageant. Scouts fed in contrived gusts at intervals, piped through the vents with Reeve's blessing and Ilex's mischief. The room rolled through the cadence as if stepping into shoes it had laced for months: *alarm → post → adjust → tend → return → revise if needed → ledger in parallel → gap check → continue.* Delegates watched chalk precede ink by a heartbeat and realized the beat was the whole point.

The northern attendants attempted sabotage with manners. "This is theater," one said loudly, gesturing at the staged gust. "Storms are not polite."

Pip pointed at the East Wall board from storm day, chalk stains stubborn as scars. "This is not staged," she said. "We did not invent rain." She didn't raise her voice. She didn't need to. The board had more authority than volume.

An eastern envoy tried to trip them with an edge case. "If a worker posts a lie out of fear, do you punish?"

"We revise," Sera said. "Then we ask why fear taught lying better than posting. That question belongs to leaders, not the worker."

A compact queen asked something practical. "If our ledgers lag, how do we survive the envy of auditors?"

The senior auditor, who had chosen humility as a second career, answered. "Make ink walk beside chalk. Not ahead. Then call delay failure. We learned to love *so far.* Teach them that."

The room softened around the words. *So far* traveled like a hand signal.

After the drill, delegations queued at the boards the way pilgrims queue for water. Some copied with care. Some snapped opinions instead of notes. A few left frowning, because dullness could not be sold at a premium. Dullness, finally, was their pitch.

Sable opened a fresh page in the archive: Forum Corrections. He wrote down the northern envoy's accusation and the exact revision that answered it. Beneath, he logged the compact as policy with three words that smelled like permanence: *posted at doors.*

Vetch watched the exits. The rumor-bearers left first, unsatisfied. The learners lingered. He let them. Guards in this hive guarded time more than thresholds.

On the way out, a young visitor from the east slipped a folded wax into Blair's hand. Inside: two lines, cramped and urgent. *Queen forbids boards. Workers want them. Advise?*

Blair wrote back on the same scrap and folded it to the same crease. *Start small. Post tend times on your own cell. Call gaps on your corridor door. Use so far. Bring guards when you can. Teach numbers. Storm will argue for you.*

The courier tucked the plan beneath a wing like an amulet that didn't need blessing.

Evening cooled the room into usefulness. The queen closed the forum with no flourish: "We have shown what we can share. We have named what we cannot sell. The meadow will decide what it believes when weather visits."

As delegates drifted out, the northern attendants rallied one more insult: "Your windows are a fad."

Blair looked at the East Wall. "Our windows learned a season," she said. "Fads don't like rain."

The attendants left, their rumor a little thinner.

Pip exhaled the way you do when you've been speaking plain for hours. "They wanted a spectacle," she said, smiling crooked. "We gave them a rehearsal schedule."

"The only show storms attend," Ilex added, wiping torque from his hands.

Sera rewrote a smudged 3m04 without commentary. The senior auditor copied it below without rank. Reeve drew a small bridge in the compact's margin, because some symbols deserve to live.

The compact fluttered once in a draft, then settled. *Shareable/Non-Shareable* had become law not because the queen said it, but because the boards believed it.

Outside, the meadow practiced dusk. Inside, the hive practiced morning.

The smear arrived braided—rumor wound into pamphlet wound into proclamation. A flock of couriers scattered it across the meadow at once: *Window cult exposed.* Subheads marched like ants: *Workers coerced to self-denounce, Boards falsified for prestige, Numbers worshipped like idols.* The pamphlet wore a mirror on its cover and added the line, *Real hives rely on discipline, not chalk.*

Noise admired itself. Then it tried to colonize rooms.

Delegates who had stayed to learn found themselves accused of treason. Two visiting workers flinched at the word *cult* and tucked their chalk behind their backs as if it could incriminate them.

The northern attendants strutted, crown-light flashing, as if weather bowed to press releases.

The queen didn't call a counter-proclamation. She pointed to a sentence on the compact instead: Cross-Posting in Storms. "If rumor is weather," she said, "then we treat it like weather." She looked to Blair. "Run *Gap Watch* in daylight. Across hives. Let questions stand where wind can see them."

Blair felt the fear that comes with being right too early and wrong too publicly. She answered it with scheduling. "Three hives," she said. "Us, the southern queen, the compact trio. One hour. Live posts mirrored across boards. No speeches. Corrections welcome."

"Invite the rumor-bearers," Sable added. "Give them front-row boredom."

Vetch smiled, a small, satisfied hinge. "And guards at doors—not for show, for time."

They posted the hour on three meadows and six doors. The smear's pamphlets rustled on the grass like leaves pretending to be policy. Workers stepped over them the way houses step over their own shadows.

At noon, the corridor filled with watching that wasn't worship: queens, clerks, refugees, skeptics, a boy with his first dew vial, a girl with a piece of twine.

Blair raised her hand—not as priest, as metronome. "We begin with nothing," she said. "If weather comes, we count its steps."

The southern queen's board glowed on a stand beside theirs—chalk fresh, ledger open. The trio of compact hives propped a joint board labeled neighbors with a hand that looked proud to be useful.

A runner jogged in from the meadow with the first "gust"—Reeve's contrived test, honest in its intent. Pip nodded once and marked alarm—wind shift. Ilex adjusted a vent half-click. Sera tended a staged wobble. Kel returned on cue, a little shaky, a little proud. The live ledger wrote second. Rumor had nothing to eat.

A skeptic shouted from the back, pamphlet raised high. "Anyone can fake this!"

Blair pointed to the *neighbors* board. "Then watch their boards echo ours. Watch time refuse to lie."

The southern queen posted the same alarm in her hand, one breath later. The trio's board added it with the note so far and drew a tiny clock that did not ask permission to tick.

A northern attendant scoffed. “Coordination could be collusion.”

“Storms collude with no one,” Ilex said, calm as torque. “They collaborate with physics.”

Halfway through the hour, a real gust wandered in uninvited—small, contrary, unstageable. The boards changed register: alarm—wind shift (real). Sera’s posture changed by inches; Vetch’s stance by none; the room’s breath by a measurable amount. Pip posted *Tend 24s/ Return 3m14* and nested a correction beneath it: 24 → 25 with a dot like humility.

The southern queen posted her own stumble: Tend 33s (circle) target <30s. A murmur crossed the room—approval for a queen’s correction that didn’t need to court applause. The trio of hives added Gap 2m (our board smudged) and circled so far. They posted the gap’s cause: *fear.* Then the fix: *guard at door (time only).*

A pamphleteer yelled, last arrow: “This is performance! Where is the heavy weather?”

Sable, who had been writing a transcript that refused to be entertaining, pointed at the East Wall board from storm day and read the boring poetry of survival: Variance 26 → 21; Aux brace engaged; Gap log—0 so far; Revisions—5; Alarms—7. He placed the transcript next to the smear with the serenity of a librarian shelving a bad book near a better one. Audience drifted toward the shelf that wouldn’t lie.

The rumor, deprived of spectacle, coughed itself smaller.

Still, noise is stubborn. It tried an alley gate: *Workers compelled to recant.* The accusation arrived on the lips of a polished envoy who looked disappointed that nothing was on fire. “Confess,” he hissed at Kel. “Admit that you were forced.”

Kel blinked. He had flown storms and worse than storms. He lifted chalk like a witness holding his own oath. He wrote one line at knee height, for sweepers and those who crouch to repair: I returned because they posted in time. He put a dot after *time* and set the chalk down.

Sera didn’t frame it as testimony. Ilex didn’t call it a data point. Blair didn’t announce it to the room. The sentence lived without a podium. The envoy’s face performed ten seconds of indignation, then learned a new expression: irrelevance.

The southern queen stepped to the neighbors board and wrote: Our guard protected posting today. Outcome: fear fell 3 degrees.

She grinned at Vetch. Vetch nodded like a door being thanked for opening in the right direction.

The trio of hives posted a tiny correction in a tidy hand that made truth look beautiful on accident: 3m09 → 3m12 (timer). Someone in the back clapped once, then apologized to the air for being moved by dullness.

When the hour ended, numbers did not. They never do. But the demonstration wrapped itself neatly—chalk first, ink second, questions third. The queen stood where anyone standing could be seen without standing higher.

"We are not a cult," she said, voice even. "We are a house. Houses survive when they count while wind argues. We will share our ladders. We will not sell our windows. We will write corrections where everyone can trip over them. We will treat rumor as weather—log gaps, post returns, revise in light, protect the board."

She pointed to *What Travels* and *What Doesn't.* "If you want banners, you will not find them here. If you want practice, you will be bored enough to live."

The pamphlets did not ignite. They paled. That was enough.

Evening brought something that felt like a hinge clicking into a new groove. The compact trio proposed a *rolling watch*: whenever one hive faced a storm, the others would post a mirrored column titled with you—their doors becoming temporary annexes for each other's truth. The southern queen added a line: if one board washes clean, the others lend a wall. The queen signed both with small letters and no crest.

Blair gathered the field kit: one-page *Ledger & Clock,* chalk, stylus, twine, dew, guard card, consent slips, gap slate. She set three kits at the threshold with tags: south, trio, east (workers). The tags looked like invitations that refused to be ornate.

Pip tied a fresh knot at five and a half, then one more tiny knot at six as a dare for a morning that would need optimism. Ilex slotted a spare wrench under the kits the way you tuck a spare truth under a speech.

Sable filed the forum transcript under *Noise and Weather* and pinned a copy on the wall beside a blank sheet labeled Next Storm—who posts where. The blank filled with names in two hours. Not ranks. Names.

Vetch checked latches. He left one deliberately easy to open. Trust, like windows, works better when it can move.

Kel lingered at the board, tracing his dot after *time* with a fingertip as if polishing a small moon.

The northern attendants left with fewer words than they brought. The rumor's chorus kept singing at the edge of the meadow, but inside the hive the key had changed. Numbers are hard to hum.

Night stretched out like a ledger that had learned not to brag. Workers swept; guards rotated; the audit team capped their ink and left their chalk nearer the door than the desk. The compact fluttered once in a draft and settled back the way resolve does.

Blair stepped to the threshold, feeling the meadow's cool talk in her face. Far off, a modest tap-tap came from the south, answered by a faint tap from the trio's fields. Not an alarm, not yet. A check-in. The sound traveled small and sincere, ladders laid across distance by rhythm alone.

"They're watching," Pip said softly.

"Good," Blair answered. "Tomorrow, we teach them to watch each other."

She set the ladder token beside the open circle and the tiny dot by *alarm*. The three shapes made a grammar she trusted: *connect, hold open, be ready*. She looked at the boards—their mess, their steadiness, their refusal to be bought—and then at the meadow that had turned from audience into network.

The storm of rumor had spent itself on boredom. The next storm would not be made of paper.

They would be ready to move windows without exporting pride, to lend clocks without inventing creeds. And beyond the meadow, something larger arranged its weight.

9
Ladders Across

The storm of rumor had passed, but the meadow still trembled with footsteps. Where once only scouts landed, now caravans of wings arrived: not just to gawk, not only to accuse, but to ask. Questions no longer came as pamphlets or speeches—they came as notes, scrawled in haste, smudged by travel, written on whatever could carry ink.

Sable pinned them in the archive under a fresh heading: Requests for Ladders.

- *How do we cross-post without councils?*
- *Can guards protect boards in hives where guards belong to queens, not workers?*
- *What happens when chalk washes away mid-storm?*
- *If we share outcomes, do we share failures too?*

The page filled until it resembled a hive wall after rain—dense, stubborn, alive.

Blair read them aloud in the circle. "They don't want frameworks," she said slowly. "They want ladders. Something to cross with, something to hold weight."

"Then we build ladders," Ilex said, shrugging as if it were carpentry, which it was.

"Not ladders for climbing," Sera cautioned. "Ladders for reaching. If we build them wrong, they become walls again."

Pip tapped her twine. "Then every rung must be a practice. Not a promise. Write *tend, return, gap, revise.* Let them step on dull words, not shiny ones."

Vetch grunted his approval. "And guards at the base. Not to own, to keep the ladder steady."

Sable wrote in the margin: *Ladders Across—begin with four rungs.*

The first rung was tested before it was carved. A courier from the southern queen arrived breathless, carrying a wax slate: their hive had

DOI: 10.1201/9781003740056-9

posted during a squall, but half the chalk had smudged before ledger could mirror it. They asked for help.

"Answer with a ladder," Blair said.

Ilex fashioned a small kit—chalk sealed in wax tubes, gap logs pre-etched with *so far*, twine with printed knots at 30 seconds and five minutes. Pip added a card: If chalk washes, post again. Revision is not shame.

Sera tucked in three dew vials. Vetch slipped in a guard card: *protect posting, not prestige.*

They handed it to the courier with no ceremony. "Not a gift," Blair said. "A tool. Post it, revise it, make it boring."

The courier bowed low, then flew as if carrying more than wax.

The second rung came when the compact trio of hives sent word: *We want to mirror each other, but we fear chaos. Whose numbers rule?*

The circle argued.

"Consensus kills time," Ilex said. "You can't vote a brace into holding."

"But if numbers conflict, who do they believe?" Sera asked.

"Both," Blair said suddenly. "Post both. Post every hand. Let corrections fight in daylight. Truth doesn't mind witnesses."

They drafted a protocol: Cross-post without reconciliation. Correction column mandatory. If two numbers disagree, post until storm resolves. Silence is worse than contradiction.

Sable copied it onto ugly wax. Pip added in chalk across the top: Noise hates numbers. Post anyway.

The trio accepted it gratefully, and for the first time the meadow hummed not with rumor but with rehearsals.

The third rung was harder. Refugees whispered of hives where guards were teeth, not doors. "How do we protect boards when guards obey crowns, not clocks?" they asked.

Vetch answered with simplicity that startled even himself. "Then guards must be chosen by boards, not by crowns."

The circle froze.

"Explain," Blair said softly.

"Any hive can appoint one worker per corridor," Vetch said. "Not the strongest. The most stubborn. Their oath is to the board, not the throne. If crowns object, tell them storms will not wait for permission."

"Will hives accept that?" Sera asked.

"Storms will," Vetch said.

They wrote it plain: Guard Charter—oath to board, protect posting, never punish correction, never seal windows.

It traveled faster than rumor. Workers memorized it before councils could forbid it.

The fourth rung emerged almost accidentally. A young visitor asked, timidly, "When we cross-post, do we share failures too? Or only victories?"

The room went quiet.

Finally Blair answered. "Failures are the strongest rung. If we hide them, ladders break."

Sera wrote on the wall: Failure posted = trust. Failure hidden = collapse.

Kel stepped forward, steady at last, and scrawled in thick strokes: I spilled twice before I learned to return. My hive called it weakness. This hive called it practice.

The words spread before the ink dried. Refugees copied them onto wings with soot. The southern queen pinned them to her own board, crown level with chalk.

The meadow, which grades faster than councils, nodded without applause.

By dusk, the first ladder stood: four rungs, not polished, not fragile.

- Practice over promise (tend, return, gap, revise).
- Post contradiction (never silence).
- Guards for boards (oath to posting, not crown).
- Failures travel (trust is built on them).

Sable filed it under *Ladders Across v1.* He left margins wide, labeled *storms.*

Blair touched the page and whispered, "If these rungs hold, windows can cross without breaking."

The queen nodded. "Send them. But send them dull. Beauty is too easy to steal."

Outside, the meadow darkened into a quiet that sounded like preparation. Other hives were not done watching. Some were readying storms of envy, others storms of need.

The boards inside glowed steady, messy, stubborn. A hum rose from their hive—a note that sounded not just like survival, but like invitation.

Tomorrow the ladders would be tested. And tomorrow was already climbing toward them.

The first ladder was tested sooner than they hoped.

A courier staggered in from the compact trio of hives, wings frayed from urgency. He carried no message—he carried a board shard, chalk still clinging. "We tried," he panted. "Storm hit. Two hives posted. The third—" He broke off, trembling.

They gathered around the shard. It bore two columns side by side, numbers aligned but different: Tend 27s/31s. Return 3m18/4m01. Beneath them a blank where correction should have been.

"They silenced it," Pip said, jaw hard.

"They reconciled," the courier whispered. "Council demanded one number. Said contradiction would shame us. So they erased."

Sera closed her eyes. "Silence dressed as neatness."

Blair breathed slowly. "Then rung two failed. We must write it stronger."

That evening, the boards carried a revision. Sable wrote it plain across the top:

> Rung Two (amended): Post contradiction. Correction column mandatory. Silence = collapse. Reconciliation allowed only after storm, never during.

Pip underlined *never* until chalk squealed.

To prove it, they staged a live test. Ilex and the young auditor deliberately posted conflicting strain numbers on East Wall: Variance 19/21. Sera logged both. The revision column noted: Check tool drift. Workers saw the contradiction, shrugged, and reinforced anyway. Ten minutes later, Ilex adjusted the meter. Variance confirmed 21. The board showed correction without shame.

"Stronger rung," Blair said. "Now it can carry weight."

The courier from the trio wept a little—not grief, but the kind of relief that smells like permission.

The second test came from the south, where the queen had pinned Kel's words on her board. A storm skimmed their fields, light but real. Their guards—appointed by workers under the new charter—stood steady.

But when one correction embarrassed an overseer, he barked at the guard to erase it.

The guard refused.

The overseer shouted, threatened, brandished his sash. The guard stood. He posted instead: Overseer attempted erasure. Blocked. Gap 0.

When the storm passed, the correction remained visible. The southern queen did not punish. She pointed to it and said, "That is the rung."

The courier who carried the news back to Blair's hive was almost giddy. "They posted the failure and the refusal," he said. "The rung held."

Vetch nodded once, proud and plain. "Boards chose their guards. It worked."

The third test was quieter but cut deeper. Refugees from a far hive, uninvited, posted their failures on Blair's boards without asking. Their numbers were ugly: *Tend 2m40. Return 11m. Spill: large.*

For a moment, even Blair's hive hesitated. Hosting another hive's shame could draw rumors sharper than storms. But Pip erased nothing. She added a correction beneath: Target <30s/<5m. Spill preventable. Gap = leadership delay.

Sera touched the refugee's wing. "You are ours while you write."

Blair turned to the watching crowd. "Failures travel. They must. If they don't, ladders snap. This rung is hardest. That means it matters most."

The refugees left lighter, leaving their shame behind like ballast. The hive carried it without apology.

That night the meadow hummed differently. Instead of rumor, it carried rehearsal. From three directions came faint tap-tap patterns: *posting... so far... revise.* The ladders were climbing themselves.

But not all news was clean. Scouts reported that the northern queen had announced her own "Ladder Model": five gilded steps, all signed by overseers, corrections forbidden. She called it *Window Discipline.*

"Banners again," Sable said, not angry, only tired.

"Storm will grade her," Ilex muttered.

Blair nodded grimly. "Then rung four must be clearer. Failure posted = trust. Hidden = collapse. If we don't write it dull, she will write it pretty and sell it."

They posted the amendment in thick chalk: Failures required. Corrections honored. Pretty lies break faster than ugly truths.

The board smudged once in a draft. Pip rewrote it uglier, thicker. It looked like graffiti. It looked like survival.

The queen convened them in the east run, no crown, no chair. "Ladders are crossing," she said. "Some break, some bend, some carry. Our task is not to own them but to keep them boring enough to survive theft."

She placed a slate on the wall, pre-etched with four rungs and blank space beneath. "Add revisions as they come. Do not defend perfection. Defend usefulness."

Workers from other hives crowded close, some writing in their own scripts:

- *Rung One works. Twine helps.*
- *Rung Two failed; amendment strong.*
- *Rung Three held; guards stood.*
- *Rung Four hardest; shame heavy, needs hands.*

Blair watched them write and realized: ladders were not furniture anymore. They were chorus.

As dusk fell, the mentor appeared on the meadow's edge, wings carrying light dust from far storms.

"They tested your rungs," it said.

"They broke one," Blair admitted. "We rewrote it. Stronger."

"And what did you learn?"

"That ladders aren't built once. They are revised like boards. The strength is not in the wood. It's in the corrections."

The figure's eyes warmed. "Good. Remember: ladders invite climbing. Be wary of those who climb to stand above, not across."

Blair swallowed. "The northern queen."

The mentor inclined its head. "Storms will speak to her. Until then, teach without pride. Pride is a rung carved too thin."

It vanished, leaving the meadow to its tapping chorus.

That night, Blair added a fifth line to the slate herself: Rung Five (draft): Cross-post intent. Share what you plan, not only what you did. Storms hate surprises more than contradictions.

Pip read it, grinned, and tied a new knot at six seconds. "A dare," she said. "But a good rung."

Sable copied it into the archive, writing beneath: *Test at next storm. Revise after.*

Blair stepped back, looking at the ladder on the wall: ugly, messy, scarred, alive.

"Tomorrow," she whispered, "we climb."

The first real test of *Ladders Across* arrived not in rumor but in weather. Scouts returned panting: a stormfront pressing from the east, already hammering a cluster of hives less than a day's flight away.

The compact trio posted at once: Requesting cross-post support. Their boards showed strain and spills in numbers that smelled of fatigue. Beneath them, a single note: *Rung Two failed last storm. We will not silence contradictions again.*

The southern queen added her own call, sharp and brief: With you.

The meadow hushed. Everyone felt it: this was no rehearsal.

Blair's hive answered. Door boards were cleared, fresh columns ruled. Sable posted Cross-Post Mode Active in chalk thick enough to survive rain. Vetch stationed guards, not at walls but at boards, ready to protect postings from fear.

"Send kits," Blair ordered. "Ugly, simple, heavy with chalk." Ilex packed wax tubes; Pip added twine bundles pre-knotted; Sera filled dew vials. Couriers launched, wings loaded with boredom that might save lives.

By dusk, postings began to echo in. The trio logged Tend 37s. Return 5m52. Spill: contained. Their second hive posted Tend 31s. Return 4m10. Spill: minor. Their third, once guilty of silence, logged Tend 45s. Return 6m20. Spill: major. Correction pending.

"Contradiction alive," Sable noted, and wrote beneath: Correction column open.

Pip chalked in their stead: Correction must arrive before dawn. So far.

The board hummed with honesty even as wind pressed against distant walls.

Not all news was clean. A courier stumbled in from the eastern queen—the one who had mocked chalk as childish. He carried nothing but silence.

"They've sealed their boards," he gasped. "Council forbade postings. Workers whisper numbers but cannot write them."

Blair felt the words like a bruise. "Rung Four betrayed," she murmured.

"Storm will punish," Ilex said flatly.

But Pip slammed her fist into the board. "And workers will pay for council's pride. We can't let silence kill them."

The circle argued.

"If we cross-post without consent, we'll look like invaders," Sera warned.

"If we don't, their workers will die unseen," Pip countered.

Blair looked to the queen. "What do we do?"

The queen's face was still. "Post what they whisper. Not in their name—ours. Mark it as *heard.* Storm will know the difference."

That night, couriers carried whispers from sealed corridors. "Strain variance twenty-six," one murmured. "Return… too long." Their eyes begged more than their mouths could.

Blair's hive posted on their own board: Heard: variance 26. Heard: return >8m. Heard: spills. Correction welcome if ever allowed.

The words looked fragile, like trespass. But when the wind pressed harder, the meadow itself seemed to nod.

Vetch stood guard at the posting, daring anyone to erase it. None tried. The rumor-bearers in the back looked uneasy; even they sensed storms respected hearing more than silence.

By midnight, the compact trio's postings grew frantic. Variance 29 → 32. Spills increasing. Two corrections posted. The southern queen cross-posted in real time: Vent half-open. Return improved. Gap logged 2m.

The hive watched contradictions pile like kindling—but kindling in daylight, not in hidden rooms.

Sera whispered, "It's messy, but it's alive."

Blair nodded. "Mess saves."

Then the courier from the sealed hive returned, eyes hollow. "They call our whispers rebellion," he said. "They've stationed overseers to silence us." He held out his palms, chalk-dusted despite the ban.

Pip seized them. "You're posting here now," she said fiercely. She scrawled on the margin: Heard by hand: tend 52s. Return 9m+. Spills unlogged. Gap infinite. She signed it with a dot, no name.

The board did not flinch.

At dawn, the storm broke heavier. The trio's second hive nearly lost a brace. Their posting was raw: Brace groan audible. Variance 34. Reinforce failed. Request help.

Blair's hive cross-posted instantly. Ilex scribbled torque options. Pip wrote Aux brace: six hands. Count 3-2-1. The southern queen echoed with Tried. Reinforced. Holding so far.

The room leaned toward the numbers as if numbers could hold the wall themselves. For a moment, they did.

But from the sealed hive came only silence. Refugees whispered more fragments: *two spills, brace sagging, workers grounded.* Blair's hive logged them all under Heard.

Sera wiped her eyes. "Posting for ghosts."

"Not ghosts," Blair said. "Witnesses. Even silence must have an archive."

When the storm eased, the meadow filled with two kinds of news. The trio had survived, battered but alive, their contradictions posted and corrected. The southern queen's board glowed with cross-posts that looked like scars, proud and plain.

The sealed hive? No postings. No couriers returned. Only silence, which felt heavier than wind.

Refugees wept into chalk dust, writing lines no council had blessed: Tend times too slow. Braces weak. Leadership deaf.

Blair's hive posted them anyway. "Failures travel," she said. "Even if the hive that birthed them will not."

The queen pinned a note beside it: Silence is collapse. Posting is survival. The storm has graded.

That night, the circle gathered. The ladder on the wall looked older, tested.

"Rung Two held after revision," Ilex said. "Contradictions saved lives."

"Rung Three held too," Sera added. "Guards chose boards, not crowns."

"Rung Four broke," Pip said bitterly. "Silence killed."

"Then we carve it deeper," Blair said. She took chalk and wrote across the rung: Failures and whispers both must travel. If crowns forbid, boards outside will post. Better trespass than death.

The words glared, harsh but needed.

Sable copied them to the archive, titling the page *Revision Under Storm.* He left room for more amendments, because storms never end where you want.

At the edge of the meadow, the mentor appeared, wings dim from distance. "What did you learn?"

Blair faced it, rain still in her hair. "That ladders don't stop storms. They let us cross together. Some hives walked, some refused, one broke."

"And what will you do?"

"Keep posting. Even whispers. Especially whispers."

The figure's eyes flickered. "Good. But remember: ladders built high can be climbed by enemies too. Guard not only the base—guard the intent."

Blair swallowed. "We'll write it dull. We'll write it boring. We'll write it true."

The mentor faded, leaving chalk dust on the wind.

By dawn, the boards displayed a new line under *Ladders Across*: Rung Six (draft): Post intent and intent's abuse. Guard not just boards, but meaning.

Blair traced the words, exhausted but steady. "Tomorrow," she whispered, "we teach them to guard intent."

The meadow rustled like a choir waiting for a conductor. Other hives leaned in, watching. Some hopeful. Some jealous. Some afraid.

The ladder held—for now.

Envy does not arrive wearing its own name. It borrows yours.

By midweek, two distant councils announced they had "adopted Ladders Across." Their couriers carried parchment bordered in gold, rungs engraved like commandments. The language was familiar until it wasn't.

- Rung One: Practice over promise (approved by council).
- Rung Two: Contradictions posted (expires after 30 minutes).
- Rung Three: Guards chosen (from the royal registry).
- Rung Four: Failures posted (with permission).
- Rung Five: Intent declared (to authorized readers).
- Rung Six: Guard intent (meaning set by throne).

They had kept the nouns and replaced the verbs.

Pip read, snorted, and handed the parchment to Vetch. He bent it until the gold cracked, as if reminding the border who worked for whom.

"They're using our ladder as a ladder to stand above," Sera said quietly.

"Envy climbs to display," Ilex replied. "Practice climbs to cross."

Blair traced the altered rungs with one finger. "They converted boredom to pageantry," she said. "If storms come, their ink will run before the chalk can shout."

Sable pinned the counterfeit beside the real, labeling it Banner Copy in ugly hand. He left a space underneath: Corrections we would post if they ever asked. He did not expect they would.

That afternoon, the compact trio sent a different kind of message. No gold, no border. A slate with numbers and a proposal.

Proposal: Shared Governance for Cross-Posting.

- What: A rotating steward team (three hives at a time) to keep *Gap Watch* schedules, mediate contradictions, and publish a daily *So Far* sheet across participating hives.
- Who: Workers nominated by boards, not crowns.
- Where: At doors, not desks.
- Why: Because storms will outgrow any single hive's reach.

Ilex's brow went up in cautious approval. "That smells like carpentry."

Sera read the *Who* twice and nodded. "If boards nominate, care will not have to ask permission."

Pip tapped the *So Far* line with her knuckle. "That's my favorite sentence in three meadows."

Vetch tilted his head. "Stewards need a guard charter. If they drift into titles, we cut them back to jobs."

Blair felt the proposal settle in her chest like a brace placed correctly: pressure dispersed, not denied. "Shared governance that isn't a throne," she said. "We can try this."

"Try?" Sable teased. "Or practice?"

"Practice," Blair corrected herself, smiling despite the week.

The queen called a small council—not of crowns but of door keepers. They gathered in the eastern run among scuffed boards and lamps that smelled like wax and weather. The counterfeit rung parchment lay on one stool; the trio's plain slate on another. The contrast did most of the speech.

"We have two roads," the queen said. "One offers reach at the price of obedience. The other offers resilience at the price of convenience. Choose dull."

"Dull and distributed," Ilex added. "Stewards you can replace like wicks."

Sera lifted a dew vial like a tiny bell. "If stewards slow care, we pull their string."

Pip wrapped twine around her palm, then unwrapped it. "Rotate fast enough that nobody learns to pose."

Vetch folded his arms. "Charter them to protect posting, not prestige. If they host a pageant, I will escort them home."

They voted with chalk: ticks on *yes*, dots on *with guard*, triangles on *trial first*. The board became a geometry of consent. Not unanimous. Sufficient.

"Then we say yes," the queen decided. "Trial. Short. Posted."

Sable wrote the agreement on ugly wax and pinned it where it could endure being ignored by the important and used by the useful.

News of the compact leaked the way useful things do—through corridors that carry work, not influence. The counterfeit councils responded with a proclamation stamped deeper than needed: *Unauthorized governance will destabilize the meadow. Align with recognized Ladders or risk isolation.*

"Isolation?" Pip said. "From what—mirrors?"

"It's a threat," Sera cautioned. "Some hives will choose safety oversight."

"Then we invite them to watch," Blair said. "If they cannot sign, they can still see."

She posted Steward Watch—Open on the door board and added a line: Stand nearby. Read numbers. You don't need permission to learn.

Two neighboring hives sent observers within the hour. They brought no crowns, only notebooks. One wrote *so far* in their own script with a care that looked like prayer finally getting the right god.

The first day of shared governance behaved like a tool that knows what it is: simple, available, replaceable.

Steward teams—one from Blair's hive, one from the trio, one from the south—took shifts at a common board set in the meadow where rain could find it. They posted *Gap Watch* rotations, mirrored alarms, and kept a single plain sheet titled So Far with three columns: *storms, corrections, remaining unknowns.*

An envoy from a gilded council approached with the posture of permission. "Who authorizes your postings?" she demanded.

"The weather," the steward from the south said without turning her head. She chalked wind shift in the *storms* column and moved on.

The envoy's mouth pinched. "And who resolves contradictions?"

"Contradictions resolve themselves in public," the trio's steward answered, tapping the *unknowns* column. "Eventually as *corrections,* sometimes as *we were wrong.* We do not punish friction. We post it."

The envoy left with a bustle that made the meadow yawn.

By dusk, *So Far* read like an honest diary: Two storms minor. One hive smudged; posted again. Contradiction posted; resolved to 21 variances. Gap: 1h by rumor; unconfirmed. Boring, stubborn, alive.

Envy tried a sharper blade. Overnight, the gilded councils launched a copy of *So Far*—glossy, crest-heavy, printed new each dawn with numbers that fit too neatly. The title: Thus Far (Authorized). Corrections absent. Contradictions edited to coherence.

Workers laughed at the name even as they winced at the pressure it carried. Some hives wavered. Pretty lies are contagious when they promise fewer chores.

Blair's hive answered the way they answer everything: with a posting. Sable pinned *So Far* beside *Thus Far* and wrote, We prefer verbs. Pip added beneath: We prefer halves. Ilex drew a tiny wrench next to 21 → 19 and labeled it turn. Sera wrote consent deferred once, then consent given below it. Vetch underlined Gap 1h (heard) and stood there until the hour died of being watched.

The glossy sheet wilted in rain. The ugly one darkened and held.

The compact trio proposed an amendment to the steward plan after day two, the kind of fix carpenters earn: Steward shifts no longer than one storm or six hours, whichever arrives first. Fatigue, they wrote, turns stewards into statues. Statues invite pigeons.

Blair signed the change with a dot and a small ladder doodled by habit. The queen approved with two words that sounded like a hammer tapping a reliable joint: "Worn right."

They added another rule: Stewards carry no sash. Their badge is a chalk smear. The meadow learned the new insignia without instruction.

The debate Blair had been delaying finally arrived like a bill you can pay only with nerve. The trio wanted to host *So Far* from a central stand on alternating weeks. The southern queen proposed a *Commons Ledger*—a single book of cross-hive postings kept under the meadow's open sky.

"Shared ledger," Ilex said, tasting the phrase for torque. "Ink beside chalk. Everybody's. Nobody's."

Sera worried aloud. "Ink invites ownership. Whose hand holds the pen?"

"The one on duty," the southern queen replied. "And if the hand forgets humility, the others post the correction on the page itself."

Blair felt two tides in her chest. Autonomy mattered. So did scale. "If we refuse, we remain pure and small," she said. "If we accept, we risk becoming important." She grimaced. "I hate important."

"Important is a mirror," Sable said. "Useful is a ladder."

The queen listened, eyes on the meadow. "We did not open windows to admire ourselves," she said finally. "We opened them to survive and to lend. We accept the Commons Ledger—under three conditions."

She wrote them on the board as she spoke:

1. Posted at the meadow, not in any hive.
2. Corrections in the margin by any hand.
3. Every page ends with so far.

"If these terms hold," she said, "ink can walk beside chalk."

The compact trio agreed at once. The southern queen grinned. Observers nodded like bees who trust a bridge because it flexes when they step on it.

Blair exhaled, half-released, half-braced. "We risk reach," she murmured.

"We risk usefulness," the queen corrected. "It is the only risk worth taking on purpose."

At twilight, the mentor appeared not as oracle but as passerby, pausing only as long as honesty ever needs.

"You traded a wall for a field," it said.

"We're building a ledger that belongs to no throne," Blair replied.

"Guard the margins," the figure advised. "Meaning is stolen at the edges first."

Blair touched the chalk stains on her palms. "We wrote *so far* at the bottom of every page."

The mentor's wings flickered with something like pride that refuses to dress up. "Then your ladder may cross a river without learning to admire its reflection."

It was gone before gratitude could become performance.

Night lowered like a ceiling the hive had learned to trust again. On the meadow stand, the first page of the Commons Ledger lay open under a wax hood. The entry was not beautiful:

> Storm minor. Cross-post held. Contradiction posted (19/21) → resolved. Gap 1h (heard) → unconfirmed. Guards rotated. Stewards changed at six hours. So far.

Pip drew a tiny clock halo above *so far* and laughed softly at her own joke. Ilex leaned the spare wrench against the stand because some altars deserve tools, not flowers. Sera tucked two consent slips into the ledger's back pocket "for luck," which in this hive meant "for discipline." Vetch took first watch without being asked.

Blair stood with the queen a moment longer. "We gave away a little of ourselves today," she said.

"We gave away boredom," the queen answered. "May it spread like weather."

They turned toward the boards. Tomorrow would bring another storm or another rumor. Both could be handled the same way: post, revise, protect the margins.

The ladder across the meadow held. It did not admire itself. It simply connected.

The takeover arrived with ceremony because ceremony believes it can outshout practice.

At dawn, a gilded council advanced across the meadow like weather with marching orders. Attendants bore a velvet cover for the Commons Ledger, a brass lock big as a boast, and a podium that required four workers to carry and promised to make the act of writing taller.

"The ledger needs guardianship," their herald announced, voice polished enough to reflect itself. "We will ensure integrity, prevent defacement, and harmonize contradictions."

"Contradictions are not disharmony," Sable murmured. "They are the measure before the correction."

Pip stood with a stick of chalk like a small, stubborn flag. "And we already have guardians," she said, chin toward Vetch and the stewards. "They wear chalk, not brass."

The gilded envoy smiled the way lacquer cracks when it thinks no one is watching. "We recognize your… folkways," he said. "But authority must be credible. Stamps are credibility."

Ilex tapped the ledger's wood with a knuckle. "Walls prefer torque."

The envoy gestured. Attendants moved to slide the velvet over the book.

Vetch stepped forward and placed his palm on the ledger's edge, not dramatic, simply true. "This page belongs to the meadow," he said. "The meadow did not consent."

"Consent?" the envoy scoffed. "Consent complicates governance."

"Consent prevents shrapnel," Sera said, without raising her voice. "Especially when storms follow speeches."

The envoy lifted the brass lock, heavy with intention. "You cannot stop us," he said, meaning, *We have always gotten our way by being loud in public.*

"Correct," Blair said. "We will not stop you. The ledger will."

She nodded to the stewards.

The southern steward read the compact aloud without flourish: "Posted at the meadow, corrections in the margin by any hand, every page ends with *so far*." She placed the brass lock on the *margins* line and wrote: Attempted lock noted. The trio's steward added beneath: Authority presented without consent. The third steward chalked a square labeled dispute in the *unknowns* column of *So Far* and underlined it once, gently.

The gilded envoy blinked. "You cannot… you can't annotate us."

"Margins are for meaning," Sable said. "You brought meaning."

The envoy planted the podium, a little off-center, as if to colonize the ground by leaning on it. He cleared his throat. "Let the record show—"

"Let the record post," Pip corrected. She chalked gust at that moment because a minor wind arrived like a timely conspirator, flipping the velvet back so the page caught light.

The stewards began their hour as scheduled: no fanfare, no delay. Under *storms* they wrote wind shift—minor; under *corrections,* earlier variance 21→20 with Ilex's tiny wrench sketched beside it; under *unknowns,* council lock—authority? and then, after a polite pause, no.

The envoy made the mistake pageants make: he waited for silence to amplify him. Practice did not provide any.

So the guild tried spectacle. Two attendants approached the ledger with ink and seal, ready to imprint a crest on the day's page. The southern steward lifted her chalk-smudged hand. "Ink walks beside chalk," she recited. "No crest walks ahead."

"We will not alter your postings," the envoy lied with decent posture. "We will merely certify them."

"Certification that increases delay is falsification by fragrance," Sable said. He wrote the sentence small in the margin because some lines deserve to be found only by people who look.

The envoy reached; Vetch did not slap the hand away. He placed the guard card on the ledger: protect posting, not prestige. "You may write," Vetch said, "if you write like everyone else."

The envoy hesitated, unsure how to be common. He set the seal down, heavy as a habit, and took the pen the way a king might take a shovel.

He wrote: Certified.

Pip wrote beneath it: Corrected: and drew an arrow pointing nowhere. The room laughed softly—the kind of laugh you hear when a child tries on a crown and it falls over his eyes.

"Record your concern," Blair offered, not unkind. "In the *unknowns* column. Then wait with us for weather to decide."

The envoy stood, trapped in compromise—a place with no ceiling for applause.

The ledger solved the impasse the way good furniture does: by being used. Scouts arrived breathless; two hives at the meadow's edge had begun posting crosswinds. The stewards moved: mirror, note, *so far.* A contradictory return time arrived—3m11 and 3m29—from the compact trio's second hive and its neighbor. Sera tapped the post both rung with a fingernail and scribbled tool drift suspected. Correction pending. A worker no one recognized added, timidly, my timer lagged to the margin with a dot and no name. The *corrections* column bloomed: 29→24 (timer); 3m11 confirmed. The ledger took the revision like a field taking rain.

The envoy tried one last blade. "You allow anonymous corrections? That invites fraud."

"Fear wrote that dot," Sera said. "And fear corrected itself. Fraud rarely improves a brace."

Ilex turned the wrench a quarter click beneath the stand and logged it because this hive preferred receipts to rhetoric.

Under *unknowns,* the southern steward wrote council role and, after a quiet five count, crossed it out. "Resolved by practice," she said, not triumphantly. Bored.

The velvet cover had fallen to the grass. A child used it as a cape long enough to learn it made running harder and abandoned it where brass could watch.

The gilded council changed tactics: if they could not own the ledger, they would star it. Their envoy announced a Grand Review, a monthly ceremony to honor the "best postings." He unfurled criteria like festoons: neatness, absence of revisions, legibility under candlelight.

Pip groaned. "A pageant for truth."

Sable pinned a new card beside *So Far*: We do not give medals for breathing. The southern steward added, We do not dock points for coughs. The trio's steward wrote, We treat lungs, not posters.

The envoy sputtered, outflanked by boredom.

Then the queen stepped forward, having said nothing until words could not be mistaken for decoration. "If you must hold a review," she said, "judge this: gaps posted, contradictions kept public, corrections timely, consent visible, guards present, so far at the bottom." She looked at the envoy kindly. "You may find it harder to award trophies when the winners are dull."

The envoy withdrew, bruised by plainness.

The ledger asked for no victory lap. It demanded maintenance. Rain flirted with the edges; Vetch adjusted the hood. A bee with clean hands rewrote a smudge at the page's foot where *so far* had absorbed too much weather. The line reappeared crisp as a metronome.

Afternoon brought an honest test. A mid-meadow hive posted a spill and blamed *gust anomaly.* Their neighbor cross-posted and added load misjudged. Contradiction crouched on the page like a cat deciding whether to leave the bowl alone. The gilded envoy smiled, sensing scandal.

"Live correction," Blair said. "At the door."

They walked together—stewards, guards, envoy, onlookers—to the hive's threshold. The board showed the same two stories. Sera asked consent of the worker, received it, and listened. Ilex checked vents, then torque, then the slope of the lane. Pip posted alarm check: load surge with a knot tied right there in twine. Return time improved by a visible inch. The worker wrote my error with hands that did not shake. The steward wrote correction: misjudged and then, in smaller letters, wind aided.

Back at the ledger, the page did not choose a villain. It wrote both causes, noted the fix, and kept the *so far* unconjugated. The envoy opened his mouth to proclaim something and found the sentence had nowhere respectable to land.

"Neutrality," Sable said, his voice like a shelf. "Not of opinion—of procedure."

The envoy's shoulders lowered, not in permission, in gravity.

Evening came with the gentleness of something that had no interest in applause. The gilded council gathered their velvet and lock and podium, which looked heavier now that function had refused them. Before they left, the envoy surprised himself by placing his seal in the ledger's back pocket—not pressed on paper, just placed like a tool being retired. "For the margins," he muttered, and left before anyone could make meaning of it.

The stewards posted the day's last line: So far unchanged.

The page breathed back a little shine.

Later, in the archive, the circle slumped into the good fatigue earned by low theater and high utility. Sable labeled the folder Ledger, Commons—attempted capture; repelled by procedure. He added a stub of brass to the pouch of artifacts, next to a broken knot of twine and a pen that had learned humility.

Pip leaned on Blair's shoulder. "We need more than ladders," she said. "We need something that winds this without us yelling."

"Engines," Ilex said, with a grin a wrench would understand. "Engines of boredom."

Sera smiled. "Devices that keep clocks honest without a queen in the room."

Vetch nodded approval he rarely spent. "Engines I can guard."

The queen closed the ledger with two hands, then set it back under the hood. "Then tomorrow we build them," she said. "Mechanisms that make practice inevitable."

Blair set the open circle and the ladder token on the table and added a tiny gear—a twisted paperclip Sable had bent as a joke and an omen. The shapes together made a sentence the hive could read without translation: hold open, connect, keep turning.

Outside, the meadow tried on night. In the distance, hives tapped a patient rhythm—check-ins, not alarms. The ledger stood under its hood like a lantern convinced of its purpose.

Blair looked once more at the page, at the bottom line that refused to become a boast.

So far.

She exhaled. The hum thickened. Tomorrow, they would begin Chapter 10: Engines of Boredom—ratchets and routines, fixtures and fail safes, the quiet machinery that makes windows and clocks run when nobody's watching.

The meadow didn't clap. It didn't need to. It was listening for work.

10
Engines of Boredom

Storms teach urgency. Rumors teach defense. But nothing teaches permanence except boredom.

The hive woke into quiet weather, the kind that makes adrenaline look foolish. For the first time in seasons, no envoys hovered, no pamphlets arrived, no gust rattled braces. Workers moved with the half-speed of wings not demanded. Silence, which had once been danger, now felt like permission.

Blair gathered the circle in the archive. The boards glowed faintly, messy with yesterday's revisions, stubborn with *so far.*

"Storms will return," she said. "Rumors will return. But if practice lives only when we are afraid, it will die when we are calm. We must build engines."

"Engines?" Pip tilted her head, twine already restless in her fingers.

"Mechanisms," Blair clarified. "Processes that keep windows open, clocks wound, ladders steady—without zeal. Engines of boredom. They must run when no one remembers why."

Ilex smiled faintly. "Then carpentry is our model. Joints that hold because gravity likes them. Not because ceremony blesses them."

Sera nodded. "Care that happens on schedule, not just in storms. The body doesn't wait for a crisis to breathe."

Vetch crossed his arms. "And guards who guard dullness as seriously as they guard danger."

Sable wrote the title on a slate, ugly and plain: Engines of Boredom v1.

They began by listing what had failed in calm seasons.

- Rituals that grew until they toppled under their own weight.
- Champions who carried reforms until their wings broke.
- Boards that dimmed because chalk dried and no one thought to refill.
- Guards who grew restless when storms were quiet and invented enemies.

DOI: 10.1201/9781003740056-10

"These are engines of drama," Blair said. "We need engines of boredom."

Pip suggested the first: Rotation Clock. Every board would post shift times for stewards, guards, and scribes—not by name, but by role. Roles rotated so boredom distributed itself like pollen.

"If you never leave a ladder in one place, it won't grow moss," she said.

Sera offered the second: Consent Slips Routine. Every care interaction would have a slip, posted or deferred, even in calm. "So workers never forget the word *yes.* Boredom must learn the same respect as crisis."

Ilex drafted the third: Torque Audit Weekly. Not ceremonial, not grand. Just a checklist: brace, vent, load, turn, log. "Engines love rhythm," he said. "We will give them one."

Vetch added the fourth: Guard Charter Review. Once a month, guards read their oath aloud—not in the queen's chamber, but at the board. Then they sign the ledger with chalk. Not for honor. For maintenance.

Sable copied all four beneath the heading. The list looked unremarkable. Which was the point.

The queen joined them late, reading the slate with an expression that hovered between skepticism and relief.

"You wish to enshrine dullness?" she asked.

"We wish to protect survival from memory loss," Blair replied.

The queen tapped the page. "Engines must also prevent hijacking. Who checks that these routines don't become ceremonies again?"

"Revision column," Sera answered instantly. "Every engine must have its own correction box. If boredom drifts, the drift is posted."

Pip grinned. "We'll audit the audits with chalk."

The queen smiled back, a rare sight. "Then let us name them as law, not as advice. Law dull enough to survive crowns."

She pinned the slate to the central board. At the bottom she wrote in her own hand: Failure to maintain engines = failure to prepare for storms.

It wasn't poetry. It was gravity.

The first test of boredom came quickly. A week of clear skies stretched, long and monotonous. No gusts, no rumor, no delegation. Workers grew restless.

One morning, the Recovery board was blank. The routine postings—tend averages, return checks—had not been written.

Pip frowned. "Rotation gap." She chalked Gap 6h. Reason: forget.

Sera added: Correction: steward assigned; posted late.

The ledger logged both.

At the next rotation, the board carried a new line: Reminder engine triggered. A small bell hung by the board, rung every shift until posting was made. No drama. Just boredom given teeth.

By week's end, no boards sat blank longer than an hour. Workers grumbled at the bell but obeyed.

"Engines work," Blair said. "Even when nobody cheers."

The second test was more subtle. Guards grew listless with nothing to protect. Vetch found two of them staging mock alarms, posting false spills to stay sharp.

"This is how zeal turns feral," he muttered.

He called the guards together at the East Wall and made them read their charter aloud: *Protect posting, not prestige. Defend boards, not crowns. Guard gaps, not gossip.* Then he had them sign chalk under their oath.

The act felt flat, unremarkable. But the next day, no false alarms appeared.

"Engines correct drift," Vetch said. "They remind guards that dullness is their duty."

Sera reported the third test: consent slips piling unused in a drawer. "Workers forget to ask when life is calm," she said.

She posted a routine at the Recovery board: Consent Check—random daily. Any care action without a slip was logged as a gap. The first day revealed three. The slips were filled retroactively, but the shame of backlog bit harder than any lecture.

"Engines keep the word alive," Sera said. "Even when crisis sleeps."

By month's end, the engines had teeth. Rotation posted without prompting. Torque checks logged weekly. Consent slips filled even in boredom. Guards signed their oaths like clockwork.

Delegates who visited scoffed. "Why waste chalk on nothing?" one asked.

"Because nothing becomes storm if left unattended," Blair replied.

She pointed to the revision columns already littered with corrections: Gap logged late. Steward replaced. Torque corrected. Consent slip misfiled. Each tiny failure posted, corrected, boring.

The envoy frowned. "This is not inspiring."

"Good," Blair said. "Inspiration is a storm. We prefer schedules."

That night, the mentor appeared on the meadow, wings quiet, as if not to disturb the calm.

"You have built engines," it said.

"They are dull," Blair admitted.

"Dull is difficult to corrupt," the figure replied. "Engines of boredom keep windows open when zeal runs dry. Storms will still test you. But now storms will meet practice that does not need drama."

Blair nodded. "We made correction boxes for the engines themselves."

The mentor smiled faintly. "Then your boredom has learned humility. That is the hardest engine of all."

It vanished, leaving the meadow to its quiet.

Blair returned to the hive and walked past the boards. They looked plain, almost tired. Numbers ticked along, gaps logged, corrections scribbled. Nothing dramatic. Nothing glorious.

She realized with a start: this was the most beautiful sight yet.

The engines had started to turn.

Engines, once built, attract tampering. Boredom irritates envy.

The first crack appeared in *Rotation Clock.* A steward from a visiting hive claimed to have completed two shifts in one—double duty, no gap, maximum efficiency. On paper it looked perfect: no blank spaces, no missed posts. But when Sable examined the ledger, he found something suspicious. Two corrections had been skipped, three alarms unlogged, and the revision column untouched.

"Perfection is the sound of silence," he muttered. "Which is also the sound of lying."

He posted a correction himself: Rotation falsified. Gap 3h. Outcomes unlogged. Correction: steward replaced.

The steward blustered, shouting about reputation. Pip leaned close, twine cutting into her palm. "Engines are not for medals. They are for minutes. You cheated time."

The steward left red-faced, but the posting stayed. The board wore it without shame, ugly and honest.

The next breach came in *Torque Audit Weekly.* A delegation from the gilded councils staged their own "audit" in front of witnesses, dramatic as theater. They tightened three vents that weren't loose, stamped seals, and declared, "Braces secured. Risk eliminated."

Ilex scowled. "They've turned wrench into wand."

He posted directly on the wall: Audit staged. Torque unchanged. Correction: retest required. Then he climbed the brace himself, tested every vent, and logged real numbers.

The difference was plain: their ink claimed certainty; his chalk showed variance. The workers believed the chalk.

"Engines are carpentry, not magic," Ilex told the crowd. "Storms don't bow to ceremonies."

The crowd nodded. The gilded envoys packed up their seals, muttering.

The most subtle attack targeted *Consent Slips Routine.* An envoy suggested replacing paper slips with pre-stamped approvals. "Efficiency," she argued. "Workers need not pause to ask; permission can be assumed."

Sera stood very still. "Permission assumed is permission denied."

The envoy waved her off. "You risk delay."

Sera held up a slip from that morning: *Deferred. Worker said not yet. Re-attempted two hours later. Consent given.* She set it on the board. "Delay protected her wings. Engines that erase delay erase humanity."

The envoy scoffed, but workers nodded. A refugee from the sealed hive whispered, "We were told consent was chaos. That lie killed us."

The envoy left quickly, the lie too raw to sell.

Vetch discovered the fourth attack when a rumor spread that guards were planning a coup. He traced it to a visitor from a northern corridor who had quietly replaced a guard's signature with a forgery.

The forgery looked neat, flawless. It fooled no one.

Vetch posted on the board: Signature falsified. Guard charter intact. Correction logged. Then he summoned the guards and had each re-sign their oath in messy chalk lines. "Engines are not calligraphy," he told the room. "They are scars. Better crooked truth than straight lies."

The forged signature remained visible as a lesson. The room respected it more than the tidy forgeries.

The queen convened the Outcomes Board. "Engines work, but envy adapts," she said. "They will counterfeit boredom. They will weaponize dullness. We must design corrections for the corrections."

Sable proposed a solution: Shadow Column. Every engine posting would have a second column where any observer—worker, steward, refugee, even skeptic—could log *Observed Drift.* No permission needed.

"Even envy can post," he explained. "Noise will drown itself in contradictions. Practice will surface truth."

They tested it the next day. A worker wrote: Observed drift: torque audit rushed. Ilex confirmed and logged: Correction: retest complete. The shadow column glowed with proof that dullness had a witness.

Soon the boards looked busier. Not dramatic, just layered: rotations, audits, consent slips, guard reviews, each with a shadow column beside them. Scribbles filled the margins: Observed drift: bell not rung. Observed drift: steward late. Observed drift: correction delayed.

Some were petty. Some were real. All were visible.

Envoys scoffed. "Your engines are clogged with noise."

Blair shrugged. "Noise posted is safer than noise whispered. Let corrections prove themselves."

And they did. Workers corrected small slips quickly. Gaps shrank. Engines turned smoother. Noise that couldn't withstand daylight evaporated.

Then came the deliberate sabotage. A gilded council posted a forged *So Far* sheet showing perfect compliance: zero gaps, zero corrections, flawless timing. They distributed copies across the meadow, declaring, "This is the true Ledger of Engines."

The hive answered with a simple comparison. Sable pinned their *So Far* beside the forgery. Theirs was ugly: gaps marked, corrections messy, shadow columns littered with complaints.

"Which looks lived?" Blair asked the crowd.

Workers pointed to the ugly sheet. "This one smells like practice," a refugee said. "The other smells like fear."

The forgery withered under rain. The ugly sheet held.

The queen addressed the hive the next morning. "Engines are not perfect," she said. "Perfection is proof of fraud. Real engines cough, correct, and continue. Boredom is noisy. We will protect that noise."

She added a line to the law: If engines produce silence, treat it as failure. Dullness must breathe.

Pip laughed. "So far has a heartbeat now."

Sera tapped the revision column. "Then let's listen."

That evening, the mentor appeared in the meadow, wings dim as if exhausted from traveling envy's terrain.

"They tamper," it said simply.

"They always will," Blair replied. "So we made shadow columns. Anyone can post drift. Even lies expose themselves when posted."

"And what did you learn?"

"That boredom needs witnesses. Engines alone are not enough. They must be public, layered, corrected by hands that do not need permission."

The figure nodded. "Then your engines are not idols. They are instruments. And instruments tune themselves in practice."

Blair smiled faintly. "We're teaching boredom to sing off-key until it finds its pitch."

The mentor's wings flickered once, like applause too modest to admit itself, and it vanished.

By nightfall, the hive felt steadier. Not because storms had ceased or rumors had died, but because engines hummed beneath everything: bells for rotations, slips for consent, torque audits posted, guards signing crooked names, shadow columns scribbled with drift.

The boards looked crowded, messy, almost ridiculous. But every smudge was proof of life.

Blair walked the corridor, hand trailing the chalk dust, whispering to herself: "Storms will come. Envy will come. But boredom will hold the wall."

And the wall hummed back, low and steady, like a machine that had finally learned its purpose.

Engines, once humming, risk becoming cages.

After three weeks of quiet storms and loud schedules, murmurs spread through the corridors. Workers grumbled at bells that rang too often, slips that felt redundant, rotations that moved too quickly for friendships to settle.

One evening, a flyer scrawled at the base of the Recovery board: We are drowning in chalk.

The sentence was neither false nor malicious. It was exhaustion written in dust.

Blair read it aloud to the circle. "Engines work," she said, "but workers feel smothered."

"They're right," Sera admitted. "Consent slips every hour make care sound like bureaucracy."

"Torque audits weekly are necessary," Ilex countered. "But perhaps we count too much when walls aren't groaning."

"Engines must protect without choking," Pip said. She tugged her twine and sighed. "Even boredom needs breathing room."

Sable wrote on the slate: Engines must hum, not shout.

The first adjustment came in *Rotation Clock.* Stewards complained that bells interrupted more than they reminded. Vetch proposed a compromise: Silent Bell. Instead of ringing each shift, the bell's clapper was chalked. Each steward marked the clapper with a tick when posting was complete.

"No sound," Vetch explained. "Only sight. The board itself keeps time."

Workers liked it immediately. No ringing, no scolding—just ticks accumulating like quiet footsteps. If ticks went missing, anyone could add an *Observed Drift* in the shadow column.

"Engines breathe easier," Blair said, watching the board.

The second adjustment came in *Consent Slips Routine.* Sera admitted the slips had become rote. "Workers sign without thinking. It's paper, not practice."

She redesigned the slips into two halves: Yes, and Not Yet. Workers tore one side off depending on their answer and posted it directly. The board filled with half-slips, a visible rhythm of consent and delay.

"Now refusal is as visible as agreement," Sera said. "And both are ordinary."

Refugees wept at the sight. "We were taught to hide 'not yet,'" one said. "You make it normal."

The third adjustment came in *Torque Audit Weekly.* Ilex realized some braces didn't need weekly checks, others needed more.

He created a Variable Audit Engine: color-coded marks beside each brace—red for weekly, yellow for biweekly, green for monthly.

"Engines adapt," he said. "Otherwise they become idols."

At first workers balked—too complicated, too many colors. But when the board posted results—green braces logged steady, red ones corrected faster—they saw rhythm, not clutter.

"Engines hum to different notes," Pip said. "That's music, not noise."

The queen watched all these revisions with a wary eye. "Engines keep you safe," she said, "but if they multiply, they become ceremony in disguise."

Blair agreed. "We must prune engines as we prune rituals."

They created a new rule: Every engine faces review quarterly. If no storm proves it useful, it is retired.

The first to go was an overzealous audit called *Lantern Check*—workers had been logging lamp brightness nightly. "We don't need engines for candles," Pip joked. The board posted *Lantern Check retired,* and workers cheered.

"Engines die, too," Sable noted. "And their funerals must be dull."

Pushback didn't vanish. Some workers still felt watched too closely. One scrawled: Engines turn us into cogs.

Blair read it aloud at the next gathering. "They are right to feel that. Engines risk turning practice into prison."

"What do we do?" Sera asked.

Blair considered. "We must give workers a say in engines. Not only stewards. Not only us. Everyone."

They created Engine Forum Days—once per season, any worker could propose, revise, or retire an engine. Proposals went straight to the board. If three corrections logged the same complaint, the engine was altered.

The first forum killed a redundant posting rule. The second added a small engine: Stretch Breaks every two hours. Pip laughed. "Even boredom needs exercise."

The hive laughed with her. The engine went up.

Not all were convinced. An envoy from the gilded councils sneered during a forum. "Your hive lets workers edit law with chalk. That is anarchy."

Vetch corrected him. "That is maintenance."

Blair added in the shadow column: Observed Drift: outsiders call practice chaos. Correction: storms call it survival.

The envoy left unimpressed. The board remained unimpressed with him.

The mentor appeared at dusk, wings faint with evening. "Engines hum," it said. "But engines also weary. What have you learned?"

"That engines need pruning," Blair answered. "And permission. Without both, they become cages."

"Good," the figure said. "Engines of boredom must never forget they serve life. If they stop listening, they are only mirrors with gears."

Pip tugged her twine. "We built shadow columns even for engines. Workers write when engines choke them. We correct."

The mentor nodded. "Then boredom has found balance. Remember: storms are dramatic, but they are rare. Engines keep truth alive in the years between."

It vanished, leaving behind a silence that felt steady instead of empty.

That night Blair walked past the boards. She saw ticks on the Silent Bell, half-slips of *Not Yet,* red-yellow-green torque marks, guards' crooked signatures, shadow columns littered with complaints and corrections.

The boards looked messy, busy, alive. Not dramatic. Not crushing. Just turning, like gears in a hive too humble to call itself a machine.

She whispered to herself, "Engines must hum, not shout."

The hum of the hive answered, low and steady, like boredom made holy.

The storm arrived with no rumor to escort it. Mid-season, middle shift, the kind of day boredom thinks it owns. A thin line of cloud pressed in from the west, unimportant until it wasn't. Wind gathered not in gusts but in a long, patient hand.

The boards did not blink. The Silent Bell clapper wore its ticks for the hour—steward signed, guard signed, ledger mirrored. No one shouted. The engines spoke first.

Pip saw the first change as a smudge at the top edge of the East Wall board—dust lifting where dust should sit. She tapped the clapper with a fresh tick, not to ring, to mark: postings current. Then she wrote the word that wakes practice without waking panic: alarm.

Ilex ran his palm along wax. The red-yellow-green marks he'd painted on braces stopped being decoration and started being triage. "Red first," he said. "Yellow on interval. Green after."

Sera slipped half-slips into her pocket—Yes and Not Yet—like breath made paper. Vetch moved to the board, the way doors move to their frames when a house learns wind.

The first tend arrived off-tempo—a flyer cut sideways by the long hand of air. Sera met her mid-lane. "Consent?" The flyer swallowed and tore Yes clean. Tend 23s went up with a stub of chalk; Return 3m12 followed on the same line as if they'd rehearsed their friendship.

The Shadow Column found its purpose. A worker scrawled Observed drift: bell ticks late; the steward added a tick and wrote correction made in a hand that looked relieved to be ordinary.

"Variance nineteen," the young auditor posted, chalk already gray to the bone. "Holding so far."

No trumpet, no sermon. The engines breathed.

The wind leaned harder. The red braces—the ones meant for weekly torque—complained in a voice the wall reserves for honest relationships. Ilex didn't reach for a general wrench; he reached for the Variable Audit map and called out turns by color.

"Brace R4—quarter turn on count. R3 no move. R2 check the vent first."

Pip echoed along the boards: 3—2—1—turn. The wall exhaled to a number. Variance eighteen. Someone smiled without meaning to, then stopped because storms dislike being mocked.

The Commons Ledger hood flapped and settled; the stewards on duty wrote wind shift—real under *storms,* then mirrored East Wall's numbers with the same bored pen they used for calm. A visiting envoy began to frame a question and abandoned it in the face of a ledger that refused choreography.

"Yellow in two," Ilex said, reading the scheme he'd painted months ago for a day like this.

"Consent?" Sera asked again to a different flyer whose eyes darted like birds trapped in a room. The half-slip Not Yet tore crisp and visible. She posted it next to Yes without hierarchy. "Deferred," she wrote. "Revisit 2m." The corridor's heart rate eased by a small, real notch.

A refugee from the sealed hive stood with both hands on her own shoulders, watching that Not Yet hang without punishment. She whispered, "This engine would've saved us."

Sera heard and put the extra half-slip in her palm. "Then it will save someone today."

The first test of zeal versus engine found Pip's voice. Her throat wanted to raise itself; the Silent Bell kept it down. She tapped another tick and wrote rotation ongoing. The clock in the corner—the one nobody admired because it was ugly enough to live—turned.

A hardliner without the old sash but with its memory edged up. "Seal the auxiliary slit," he urged. "Less air, less risk."

"Engines say leave it," Vetch answered, not with rank, with paper. He tapped the Guard Charter Review posted last week: *protect posting; do not restrict visibility without posted cause.* "Cause?"

The hardliner looked at the numbers and found no stage to stand on. "Right," he muttered. He stayed and held a span instead, which is how some loyalties learn their new jobs.

"Variance twenty," the auditor wrote. "Rising." He didn't flinch. He underlined so far. The underline was a reminder, not an ornament.

The Shadow Column caught more drift. Observed: steward late to mid-shift handoff. The steward wrote acknowledged and pointed at the Silent Bell clapper now thick with chalk ticks like tree rings. When engines miss, engines admit.

Wind sided with physics and found the brace joint Ilex had labeled a risk in spring—the circle with a narrow bridge: old patch meets new. The wall told a truth that was not yet a failure; Ilex heard it with his hands. "Aux span here," he said. "Six hands."

Workers took places without narrative. Pip counted. Sera stood not to bless but to check breath. Vetch kept the corridor's shape while bodies moved to be useful. The span rose, the wall softened, the number turned backward in small, decent increments. Nineteen. Eighteen.

"Ledger?" Blair called to the meadow stand without looking away.

"So far," the southern steward said, loud enough for weather, quiet enough for people. The page absorbed the day like bread absorbs soup.

A squall tried mischief. Rain needled in sideways and erased Return 3m12 to a blur. No one cursed. Pip wrote it again. The engine did not ask for drama; it asked for repetition.

The Engine Forum rule—rare, but alive—saved a second slip. A worker posted observed drift: consent box empty in the shadow column; Sera reached into her pocket and shook the stack in public.

The flyer who'd posted Not Yet earlier nodded like seeing your own house lights on after evening.

Ilex shifted to the yellow braces—a click here, a check there, each written because the engine cared more about receipts than charisma. "Green holds," he noted, and the board carried no action with the dignity of nothing done for the right reason.

The hardliner, now a span-holder, breathed with the count. You could see it in his shoulders: engines were teaching even his zeal how to keep time.

Midday slid with the wind and the hive learned the truth of the chapter's name. The engines were not heroics. They were outages avoided. Gap log—0 so far wrote itself without triumph; the Shadow Column offered a half-dozen petty complaints, each answered in small script. The Silent Bell clapper collected ticks like proof of life.

A visiting clerk asked Blair softly, "How did you keep them from shouting?"

"We gave the board the voice," Blair said. "We kept ours for counting."

He looked at the half-slips pinned Yes and Not Yet side by side. "And consent?"

"We made refusal ordinary," Sera answered before Blair could. "Ordinary survives storms."

The wind pushed once more, an insult rather than an argument, and went to harass a hedge.

"Yellow complete," Ilex said. "Green reassess after meal."

"Post it," Blair said. He did. The ledger mirrored. The meadow did not applaud.

Afternoon found the engines in the part of the song where the chorus repeats until everyone knows the words. Alarm → Post → Adjust → Tend → Return → Revise → Ledger. No hurry, no lag. The Shadow Column caught one more drift—Observed: bell tick missing on late shift—and the steward added it, not defensive, just compliant. Habit was winning.

A worker from the trio of hives jogged in, soaked. "Cross-post?" she asked, already reaching for chalk.

"Neighbors board—there," Pip pointed. The worker wrote with you under the *storms* column and mirrored Variance eighteen with a neat so far that made truth look almost polite.

Vetch loosened his stance the width of a sigh. Guards are allowed to trust the things they've tested.

At last the wind let go. Not defeated—bored.

"East: seventeen," the auditor posted. He wrote unchanged in smaller letters, which in this hive counts as gratitude.

The Commons Ledger closed the entry with So far unchanged and no crest. The page dried into something that would look dull tomorrow and, therefore, be believed.

Evening gathered its tools. Sera tallied Yes and Not Yet without ranking them and wrote care given = consent honored as an arithmetic even an overseer could learn. Ilex chalked the next Variable Audit dates beneath the colors. The Silent Bell clapper held the day's ticks like a spine. The Shadow Column kept its scribbles and, beside them, the quiet satisfaction of answers.

Pip tied a new knot at five seconds and another at *not yet* just to make herself laugh. Vetch initialed the guard line crooked, pleased to be imperfect near law.

Blair stood still long enough to admit pride without letting it rent a room. "Engines held," she said. "We didn't have to become heroes."

"That's the point," the queen answered from the doorway, leaving damp footprints like signatures nobody needed to read. "Make it possible to survive without inspiration."

Blair looked at the boards—ticks, slips, colors, margins—and then at the workers walking home with the specific tired that comes from doing the right small thing in the right small time.

"Engines hummed," she said.

"They will again," Ilex replied, already planning a paint touch-up for yellow that had faded into honest smudge.

The storm—such as it was—had graded them, and the grade was unremarkable. The hive slept the way a machine rests: not off, only idling, ready.

Quiet weather lingered long enough to tempt invention. Not the gilded kind—templates.

Sable laid three blank sheets on the table, ugly by design. "If engines are to travel," he said, "they should fit on paper that refuses to posture."

Blair nodded. "No frameworks. No crests. Just stencils you can trace in chalk."

They drafted three Engine Templates—one page each, margins wide, verbs short.

1. Rotation Clock (Silent Bell)
    - What posts: who holds the hour (role, not name).
    - How: tick the clapper when postings done; if a tick is missed, anyone may add Observed Drift.
    - When: start/mid/end of shift.
    - Proof of life: visible ticks.
    - Failure mode: silence = gap.
    - Correction box: *tick added/steward replaced/reason posted.*

2. Consent Routine (Half-Slip)
    - What posts: Yes or Not Yet (tear and pin).
    - How: ask before care; post halves side by side.
    - When: always; boredom counts.
    - Proof of life: both halves present in a day.
    - Failure mode: only *Yes* appears = drift.
    - Correction box: *deferred posted/revisited/consent given or not.*

3. Variable Torque Audit (Colors)
    - What posts: red/yellow/green marks per brace; turns logged.
    - How: red weekly, yellow biweekly, green monthly; post *no action* when none.
    - When: on schedule; storms can upshift a color.
    - Proof of life: schedule visible; *no action* accepted.
    - Failure mode: decorative colors.
    - Correction box: *retest/color changed/tool drift.*

Sera added a fourth on her own initiative, eyes steady: Guard Charter Review (Crooked Signatures)

- What posts: oath lines; signatures messy on purpose.
- How: read at board, not dais; sign with chalk, not seal.
- When: monthly or after rumor.
- Proof of life: new crooked lines.
- Failure mode: perfect calligraphy.
- Correction box: *forgery found/re-signing done.*

Pip grinned and wrote at the bottom of each: so far. It looked like a hinge hiding in lowercase.

They took the pages to the door and pinned them where templates belong: next to the mess they describe.

"Send copies?" Sable asked.

"Better," Blair said. "Send blanks."

Blanks flew. Couriers carried stacks to neighbors who asked for help and to skeptics who never would but might use a page in private. The southern queen posted all four in her corridor with a note in her own hand: *Borrow, revise, return dull.*

A petty council tried to bureaucratize the gift within a day. Their proposal arrived embossed: Engine Compliance Registry—forms, inspections, fines for missing ticks, penalties for half-slips posted after dusk.

Pip read it twice and burst out laughing, the sound of a knot untying itself. "They want to grade boredom with ceremony."

Ilex tilted the paper as if to see if gravity would reject it. "It's heavy," he admitted. "But not with sense."

Sera wrote on the board beside the proposal: Observed Drift: engines threatened by registry. Correction proposed: joke + checklist.

Blair raised an eyebrow. "A joke?"

"Jokes puncture pomp," Pip said, already chalking. Under the registry notice she wrote a three-step *Engine Audit* in letters large enough to embarrass banners:

1. Look—do you see ticks? crooked signatures? two halves? colors with dates?
2. Listen—do you hear silence where a bell should be, or shouting where a tick would do?
3. Lift—can any worker lift the page and use it without permission?

"If the answer to #3 is no," she added, "burn the registry for heat."

Workers laughed the weary kind of laugh that adds years to your life. Even the queen smiled, which she saved for practical heresy.

But they still needed a counterweight. So Sable posted a one-line Commons Checklist beneath the joke:

- Posted: ticks, halves, colors, crooked names, shadow column scribbles, *so far.*

Nothing else. No signatures, no stamps. Rain-proof in spirit if not in fiber.

The registry wilted in the same weather that preserves plain paper.

With the templates pinned and the registry deflated, the hive faced a softer danger: zeal returning in bureaucrat's clothing. The engines worked so well that some stewards began inventing sub-engines to improve them: *tick-of-the-tick, half-slip index, color-brightness calibration.* Useful, maybe. Hungry, definitely.

Blair called a pruning hour. "Show us your upgrades," she said gently. "Then show us the storm that demanded them."

Silence did what it does when asked to produce weather.

"Retire them," the queen said. "Engines are shelters, not hobbies."

They retired five with a chalk line that felt like mercy. Sable wrote, Engine graveyard (visited quarterly) on a small slate and leaned it beside the archive door like a broom you shouldn't throw away but must not dance with.

Visitors kept coming, but now their questions had softened. Workers arrived with pages folded under wings, smudged in the margins with nicknames and jokes. A clerk from the east asked, shuffling his blank template, "What if our queen refuses crooked signatures?"

Vetch answered by writing his name wrong three times on the page. "Then sign wrong until it looks right," he said. "Crooked is proof of hand, not rank."

A steward from the trio asked, "Our colors confuse new flyers."

Ilex shrugged. "Use shapes," he said. "Triangles weekly, squares biweekly, circles monthly. Engines tune to the hands that hold them."

Sera helped a refugee glue a half-slip back together—Yes touching Not Yet—to carry to a hive where refusal still meant punishment. "Take the whole," she said. "Show them consent isn't copied; it's torn fresh."

Pip taught a child to tick the Silent Bell clapper with an exaggerated flourish, then erased the flourish and made her do it small. "Engines are for grown-up boredom," she said kindly. "You'll like it when you're tired."

The child nodded solemnly, as children do when they agree to become future adults in tiny installments.

The Commons Ledger learned a new habit too. Beside its daily entry, a narrow gutter appeared labeled Engine Notes. Not reports, just scraps: *ticks visible even in rain, half-slips travel poorly if not waxed, shadows need space wider than pride.* Stewards from far corridors added tips like recipes: *chalk stubs in jars by door, color legend carved into brace, guard oaths at dawn before mouths get fancy.*

None of it was inspirational. All of it was useful.

The gilded councils tried one more time, out of obligation more than hope. They proposed Engine Medals for "outstanding compliance." The medal sketch was elaborate enough to require its own guard.

Blair carried the sketch to the board and taped it there with two strips of ugly wax. Beneath it she wrote, Outstanding compliance = steady ticks on boring days. Medal awarded daily to nobody. Then she drew a little empty hook.

The joke traveled faster than the medal could.

Near dusk, with the templates posted and the last bureaucracy chuckling itself into impotence, the mentor appeared at the threshold as if checking whether boredom still admitted ghosts.

"You encoded engines," it observed.

"We resisted encoding pride," Blair answered.

"What did you learn in the encoding?"

"That travel requires blanks," Sable said from behind a lamp. "Not commandments—space."

"Also," Pip added, "that jokes are tools. They keep engines from dressing up."

"Also," Ilex said, "that shapes are just colors for hives with dim lamps."

"Also," Sera finished, "that *Not Yet* is an engine on its own."

The figure's eyes warmed. "And what image will you keep to remember this chapter?"

Blair looked at the Silent Bell clapper, dense with ticks like tree rings; the Consent halves posted side by side; the Variable colors touched up to the honesty of smudge; the Guard signatures marching crooked beneath an oath that refused to ask for a crest; the Shadow Columns full of petty complaints and decent corrections; the Commons page ending, as always, the only way that invites tomorrow.

"Hum," she said. "A roomful of it."

The mentor nodded once. "Keep humming until storms feel like interruptions, not origins."

It vanished without echo. Engines prefer exits that do not need applause.

The hive cleaned up for evening the way a kitchen does, not a stage: brushes, jars, folded blanks, dew vials counted. The Engine Templates ruffled in a draft and settled—three pages and a fourth, ugly, readable, already stained with fingerprints. A neighbor took two blanks without asking; the board considered that permission.

Vetch set his palm on the ledger hood, not to bless, to check it didn't wobble. Ilex chalked a small triangle on a brace for a new crew that hated color names. Sera pinned a fresh strip of wax beside the half-slips with a note: *for rain.* Pip made a tiny knot that meant nothing and smiled anyway.

Sable slid the day's pages into a folder stamped Engines—Living. He left a wide margin on the index and wrote Retired (funerals dull) in the corner, because organization also deserved a joke.

Blair stood in the corridor and listened. No speeches. No drums. A low, layered sound—ticks gathering, pencils scratching, quiet feet, the ledger's page breathing, a child's laugh being immediately shushed into a smile, the windy kind of peace that comes from tools put away clean.

The hum settled, not like a secret, like a standard. It did not announce safety. It produced it, one tick at a time. On the Commons page, the last line received its nightly care, rewritten where a thumb had smudged the r:

so far.

The hive exhaled as if given permission by its own handwriting.

Engines had become furniture, and furniture had become promise. Tomorrow would not need drama to work.

The meadow approved in the only language it trusts—weather less evening—and carried the templates outward.

11
The Illusion of Stability

The hum of the hive settled into its steady rhythm again.

Not strained.

Not frantic.

Just routine.

Workers moved through the corridors with practiced rhythm. Overseers updated logs. Engineers monitored the vents. The council prepared its quarterly report.

From the outside the hive looked strong.

Order had returned.

The systems were running again.

But Blair could not shake the feeling that something important was slipping away.

During the storm everyone had been paying attention.

Leaders had stayed close to the work.

Engineers had made decisions without waiting for permission.

Workers had trusted what they saw instead of what the forms required.

The hive had felt alive.

Now the rituals were returning.

Inspection tables.

Signatures.

Attestations.

Responsibility drifting slowly back into layers of process.

Sable stepped beside her near the entrance.

"You feel it too," he said.

Blair nodded.

"Yes."

"What does it feel like?"

DOI: 10.1201/9781003740056-11

Blair watched the workers moving through the inspection line.

"Distance."

Sable looked toward the council chamber.

"Distance from what?"

Blair answered without turning.

"From the work."

They stood quietly for a moment.

Pip approached a few seconds later and joined them near the entrance.

"Everything looks stable," she said.

Blair nodded.

"Yes."

Pip looked at her.

"But?"

Blair looked out toward the dark meadow beyond the hive.

"Sometimes stability means the problem is solved."

She paused.

"And sometimes it means people stopped asking questions."

The night air drifted through the entrance carrying the scent of the fields.

For the first time in weeks the hive felt calm.

No alarms.

No emergency repairs.

No one running through the corridors.

Just the steady rhythm of routine.

But Blair had lived through the storm.

She had seen what the hive looked like when people stopped waiting for instructions and started paying attention to what was happening.

She had seen how quickly things moved when responsibility stayed close to the work.

And she had seen how easily that clarity faded once the pressure disappeared.

Sable spoke quietly.

"Most hives forget."

Blair nodded.

"I know."

Pip looked between them.

"Forget what?"

Blair turned toward her.

"That the storm wasn't the problem."

Pip frowned.

"Then what was?"

Blair watched the workers finishing their final signatures before leaving for the night.

"The distance that existed before it."

Pip thought about that.

"And now?"

Blair looked back toward the quiet corridors inside the hive.

"Now we find out if anyone remembers."

The hive hummed steadily in the darkness.

Calm.

Orderly.

Predictable.

From the outside it looked like success.

But those who had lived through the storm understood something most hives eventually forget.

Stability can feel like transformation.

Sometimes it is.

Sometimes it is only the moment before drift begins again.

And the future of the hive would depend on whether anyone was still willing to notice the difference.

For Product Safety Concerns and Information please contact our EU representative GPSR@taylorandfrancis.com Taylor & Francis Verlag GmbH, Kaufingerstraße 24, 80331 München, Germany

Batch number: 10823959

Printed by Printforce, the Netherlands